THE
LITTLE GIANT®
ENCYCLOPEDIA
OF

D0733873

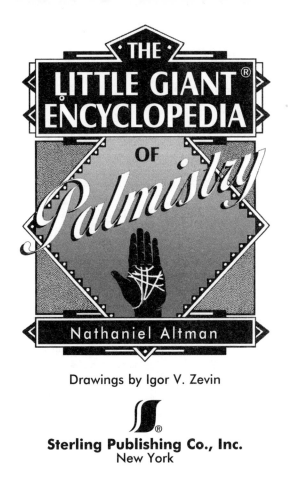

THE
LITTLE GIANT® ENCYCLOPEDIA
OF
Palmistry

Nathaniel Altman

Drawings by Igor V. Zevin

Sterling Publishing Co., Inc.
New York

Designed by Jeff Fitschen

Library of Congress Cataloging-in-Publication Data

Altman, Nathaniel. 1948-
The little giant encyclopedia of palmistry / Nathaniel
Altman: drawings by Igor V. Zevin.
    p.   cm.
Includes bibiographical references and index.
ISBN 0-8069-6161-9
Palmistry. 2. Palmistry—India. 3. Palmistry—China.
Title.
BF921.A46 1999
   133.6—dc21   98-44562
                                                              CIP

10 9 8 7 6 5 4 3 2

Published by Sterling Publishing Company, Inc.
387 Park Avenue South
New York, NY 10016–8810
© 1999 Nathaniel Altman
Distributed in Canada by Sterling Publishing
c/o Canadian Manda Group, One Atlantic Avenue, Suite 105
Toronto, Ontario, Canada M6K 3E7
Distributed in Great Britain and Europe by Cassell PLC
Wellington House, 125 Strand, London WC2R 0BB, England
Distributed in Australia by Capricorn Link (Australia) Pty Ltd.
P. O. Box 6651, Baulkham Hills, Business Centre,
NSW 2153, Australia

Sterling ISBN 0-8069-6161-9

Dedicated to the memory of

Michael Laverick

CONTENTS

PREFACE

*T*he *Little Giant Encyclopedia of Palmistry* is an authoritative yet easy to read introduction to the fascinating art and science of hand analysis.

Though still widely viewed as a form of gypsy fortune-telling, hand analysis is gradually shedding its old sideshow image. Scientists at a number of major research centers, like the Galton Laboratory at University College in London and Emory University School of Medicine in Atlanta, have investigated the medical and psychological meanings of the lines and skin ridge patterns of the hand (known as dermatoglyphics) and a growing number of articles have been published about the medical and psychological significance of hand analysis in reputable peer-reviewed journals like *The American Journal of Cardiology*, *Nature* and *Gastroenterology*. Over the past few years, a growing number of therapists have been viewing the hand as an important tool for self-knowing and have discovered that the shape, contours, lines, nails, and skin ridge patterns of the hand enable them to better understand the character traits, health, and innate talents of their clients.

In addition to revealing detailed information about your

personality, abilities, health, career, relationships, and spirituality, your hands reflect present trends and future possibilities. By making lifestyle changes and adopting new perspectives, you can actually make your lines change over time.

The book you are holding in your hands is the product of over thirty years of research and experience. While focusing primarily on the Western palmistry tradition, *The Little Giant Encyclopedia of Palmistry* also introduces the elements of traditional Indian Palmistry and Chinese Palmistry.

I

THE BASICS

1

HAND AS HOLOGRAM

When you look at your hands, what do you see? The most obvious characteristics are the fingers, the palm (along with raised areas of the hand like the thumb ball), color and texture of the skin, and at least three major lines, known as the life line, head line, and heart line. If you look more closely, you can also notice the forms of your fingers, including their relative length, thickness, flexibility, and the way they bend towards or away from each other. If you have good eyesight (or use a magnifying glass), you can examine your fingerprints, the network of smaller lines on the palm and fingers, and other patterns on the palm's surface, such as loops and whorls.

Hand in History

People have been fascinated with the hand for thousands of years. Studies of the human hand—both as a tool for creative expression and as a mirror of our inner selves—go back over five thousand years. It is believed that the Chinese began studying the hand as early as 3000 B.C. It has always been viewed as an important form of personal identification, as seen in the legal document regarding the sale of land reproduced in Figure 1.1. In India at about the same time, Aryan sages developed the study of hand analysis, *Hast Samudrika Shastra*, as part of the larger science of Samudrika Shastra, which interprets human nature and forecasts destiny by scrutinizing the forehead, face, hands, chest, and feet. Writings related to the study of the human hand can be found in Indian literature dating back to 2000 B.C., while the earliest references to palmistry itself can be found in the Vedic text, *The Laws of Manu* (vi:50).

Although no written records remain, we know that the ancient Chaldeans, Tibetans, and Babylonians studied the hand, as did the early Egyptians and Persians. Throughout the Arab world today, hand reading, known as *Ilm-ul-kaff*, is a highly respected study and avocation.

Among the early Jews, hand reading was spoken of in the *Zohar*, the ancient compendium of Kabbalistic knowledge, and references to the psychological and mystical significance of the hand have been found in early European manuscripts as well.

Figure 1.1: Handprint on legal document (China, 1753).

The ancient Greeks were enthusiastic students of hand symbolism and hand analysis, and coined the term *chirosophy* (from *xier*, hand and *sophia*, wisdom). Aristotle was supposed to have found an ancient Arabic document on chirosophy on an altar to Hermes. He is credited with having authored several specialized treatises on hands, including one written especially for Alexander the Great. Particularly interested in the markings of the hand and their significance, Aristotle wrote, in *De coelo et mundi causa*, "The lines are not written into the human hands without reason, they come from heavenly influences and man's own individuality." A drawing of a hand from a translation of his book *Chiromantia* can be seen in Figure 1.2.

In addition to Alexander the Great, Claudius Galen, Anaxagoras, Hippocrates, Artemodoros of Ephesus, and Claudius Ptolemaeus were serious students of both medical and psychological chirosophy as well as *chiromancy*, the art and science of foretelling the future by the lines of the hand.

The *Holy Bible* offers a wealth of references to the human hand and its significance. We find specific references to palmistry in Job 37:7 ("He sealeth up the hand of every man; that all men may know his work") and in Proverbs 3:16 ("Length of days *is* in her right hand; *and* in her left hand riches and honor"). Exodus 7:5 speaks of the hand as signifying God's presence and power, Ezra 7:9 as a sign of His benevolence, and Isaiah 8:11 portrays the hand as a conveyor of God's thoughts and wishes: "For the Lord

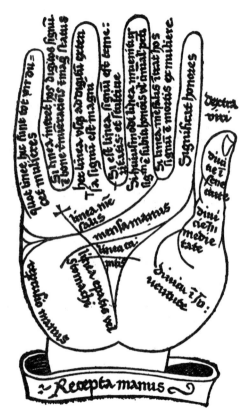

Figure 1.2: From Aristotle: *Chiromantia* (Ulm, 1490).

18

spake thus to me with a strong hand, and instructed me that I should not walk in the way of this people..."

Mirror of the Soul

The hands are vital for their ability—in conjunction with the brain—to express *who we are*. By the time we are twelve to fourteen months old, psychologists say, our hands have begun to reflect feelings of need, joy, sorrow, anger, surprise, and caring. They serve as vital components in everyday speech and enable us to express our deepest emotions to others.

The concept that our hands express who we are forms the foundation of psychologically-oriented hand analysis (chirology) as opposed to predictive palmistry or chiromancy. Although our manner of walking, facial expression, and posture all express our inner being to some extent, our hands are far more expressive, more specific, and can reflect the essence of our lives with greater depth and accuracy than any other part of the body. This fact impressed the noted Swiss psychiatrist Carl Jung to such a degree that he decided to study psycho-chirology himself. In the introduction he prepared for *The Hands of Children* by Julius Speer, Dr. Jung wrote:

...Hands, whose shape and functioning are so intimately connected with the psyche, might provide revealing, and therefore interpretable, expressions of psychological peculiarity, that is, of human character.

Why is this? As our basic instrument of touch, the hand plays a leading role in conditioning the brain, body, and emotions to develop certain responses to the world around us. In addition to being a mirror of our inherent genetic makeup, the hands can also reveal changing patterns of health, emotional stability, the development of talents, and major events, which are determined by the way we respond to our life experience.

Though thousands of years old, hand analysis is still a young and developing science. Although we still do not fully know *how* and *why* the hands reveal what they do, a complex system has evolved over the centuries that can show—through the study of the hand's shape, texture, contours, and lines—important information that can serve as a guidepost for self-understanding and personal fulfillment.

2

ORIENTATION

When we have our hands read, many questions often come to mind:

- How long will I live?
- When will I get married?
- Will I remain healthy?
- How many children will I have?
- Am I going to make lots of money?

Since the human hand has been regarded as being able to identify both present trends and future possibilities regarding health, career, personality, and relationship, many hand readers happily respond to these questions by making predictions: "You will live to be 65 years old." "You will divorce by the time you are forty." "You will have three children." "You will make tons of money."

While it is always gratifying to receive specific answers to your questions, these hand readers may actually be performing a disservice to their clients by making predictions. In addition to the possibility of being mistaken in their prediction (which takes place more often than many would care to admit), they forget the essential rules in palmistry:

1. *The hand reveals tendencies and not always definite facts,* and

2. *The lines in the hand can change over time.*

Obvious changes in the lines of the hand can be noticed over a one- or two-year period, but I have also seen major changes show up in as little as six weeks.

Like a hologram revealing several dimensions of reality, the hand can reveal our life situation in several basic ways.

- It offers us a view of the genetic makeup that we inherited from our parents, which reflects our ancestral gene pool. We can observe genetic traits not only through the size and shape of the hand, but by analyzing the fingers, nails, fingerprints, and other skin ridge patterns on the palm itself. Most of these characteristics cannot be changed, although some people can change the shape of their hand, reduce, or increase the number of lines, and alter the original strength and flexibility of their hand through certain activities, such as heavy manual labor, working with chemicals, or weightlifting, especially if these activities are performed without gloves. A good hand reader will take these factors into consideration.

- Although we come into the world with a unique collection of lines, hand flexibility, nail form and color, and mounts on the palm (scientifically known as *thenar elevations*), these features can change over time. Lines may lengthen or become shorter, appear or disappear, break or mend; mounts may become larger or smaller; nails may change color, fingers may bend (whether due to personality changes or diseases like arthritis); the color of the palm may become pale or reddish, or the hand itself may become more flexible. In some people, these features change quite dramatically, due to major events in life or major changes in attitude, thinking, or lifestyle. They may or may not be due to a change in work habits, such as moving from an office job to a job involving heavy physical labor.

By distinguishing between what is apparently "set in stone" and what can be changed over time, a reader can offer a client a balanced and genuinely useful hand analysis. For example, the life line may reveal a period of disease; in some cases, it can reveal specific health problems, such as heart disease, cancer, or food allergies.

Hand readers can deal with these signs in two ways.

They can say, "Your hand shows that you are going to have a heart attack when you are fifty years old," and leave it at that. If the reader happens to have made accurate statements before, the client will probably believe that a heart attack is inevitable at age fifty. In addition to reacting to this unfortunate news with worry and despair (which can lead to stress-related diseases such as hypertension), such clients may develop the perspective that they do not have long to live and plan accordingly. This may lead them to decide not to take care of themselves ("I'm going to die at fifty, so what's the use?"), or not to become involved in a relationship ("What's the point in getting married, since I won't be around to see my children grow up?"), or seek temporary employment as opposed to pursuing a fulfilling career.

Aware of the ever-changing nature of the human hand, a wiser hand consultant can observe the same indication and say, "If you don't take care of your health, I see a potential heart attack when you are fifty years old." Although this determination may be based on a broken life line, broken heart line, or even genetic signs, the reader understands that the hand reveals potentials *that can be changed.* A low-fat, high-fiber diet, a healthy exercise regime, abstaining from smoking and excessive drinking, stress management, and other lifestyle changes can substantially reduce the potential for an early heart attack or other health problems. In Chapter 10, we will see the handprints of a man who changed his diet and cut down on smoking, which allowed his broken life line to mend completely in only one year.

By the same token, instead of saying, "You will get divorced," a palmist can say: "If you don't work on this marriage, I can see a possible divorce." Rather than predict, "You will not have a good career," a reader can say: "You need to pay attention to your long-term career plans or I see problems ahead." Instead of "You'll become a drug abuser," a reader can advise, "You have to be especially careful of drugs, alcohol, and medications, since they can affect you more strongly than most people." By affirming that the hand shows potentials and trends, palmists may empower their clients and assist them in taking charge of their own destiny.

In some cases, lines may not change. Again, this is not to be interpreted as a wholly negative issue. In many cases, a weak, broken, or islanded line can serve as a reminder to help us focus on the area of weakness. If a person's career line continues to be weak or deficient, it does not necessarily mean that the person will have a problem in the work life: it can also be a sign that the person is not easily satisfied with work and constantly needs to focus on improving his or her career possibilities. If a union or relationship line is weak or broken, it does not always mean potential divorce: the weak line may also serve as a sign that the person must never take the relationship for granted, and should do what is possible to improve it.

While a broken, islanded, or weak line may call our

attention to a potential problem, it should not be interpreted as necessarily "bad." Very often we are confronted with challenges, choices, and difficulties in order to learn important lessons, which can be extremely valuable for us. For this reason, it is important not to judge a feature of the hand, such as a broken line or curving finger, as negative.

Unlike other books, which deal primarily with the "fortune-telling" aspects of hand reading, we will focus on hand analysis as a tool for self-knowing. This more psychologically oriented discipline of hand analysis can be of value in a number of important ways:

- Hand analysis helps people develop self-recognition on a deep level. It can indicate strengths and weaknesses, point out lessons we need to learn, and reveal major inner issues we need to resolve. It also teaches that conflict has a benign purpose in life and helps us to develop wisdom, patience, courage, and experience.

- It can offer a perspective on life that is both objective and real. Hand reading goes beyond our limited ego patterns and projections and gives us an idea of where we are in life and where we are going. It shows how our basic psychological nature can affect our health, career, and relationships, and can indicate what is needed to achieve a greater sense of harmony in our lives.

- Because palmistry often confirms our basic insights and inner feelings, it can bring a greater degree of self-confidence and self-reliance. This enables us to look at our lives with a deeper sense of ease, and helps us to work through challenges and obstacles with optimism and purpose.

- Hand analysis enables the person to determine the types of activities to pursue that will bring the greatest amount of pleasure, interest, and self-fulfillment.

- Hand analysis can reveal how our experiences fit into an overall pattern of events that constitute our basic life structure or life plan. It helps us to see life more in terms of an adventure to be experienced than an endless series of problems, obstacles, frustrations, and punishments.

- Palmistry helps those we counsel to get in touch with their deeper essence that goes beyond the ego consciousness level. It allows them to draw from this wellspring of strength and inner wisdom so that they can move more confidently through periods of difficulty.

- In addition to helping the people for whom we are reading, palmistry helps readers achieve a deeper level of inner attunement with their "clients" rather than projecting their own subconscious assumptions into what should or should not be done in their clients' lives. It helps us understand their real needs and arrive at an appropriate recommendation.

- For those who are serious about developing their knowledge of palmistry to serve others, hand analysis will help them get more deeply in touch with their own inner being, and lead them to rely more on intuition and inner wisdom in their work.

- Finally, hand analysis affirms the uniqueness and "specialness" of every single human being. No one else on the planet has a hand exactly like yours. In a culture that often encourages sameness and conformity, palmistry reveals that each individual is unique, has a special task in life, and a special combination of qualities to offer. Palmistry can help us to both understand our most important goals and find ways to attain them.

3

HAND TYPES

Over the years, many hand readers have sought to classify the hands into distinct categories. Some are based on the four elements, such as earth, fire, water, and air, or on different shapes of the hand, such as square, spatulate, or conic. While no system is perfect—and few hands actually conform to one specific hand type—classifying them gives us a general framework on which we can build a thorough hand analysis.

The system of hand shapes we will be using in this book is based partly on the "six hand types" introduced by Cheiro (1866–1936), the famous Victorian palmist and seer. He based his system on one developed by the French palmist Captain Stanislaus d'Arpentigny, whose book *The Science of the Hand*, translated by Ed. Heron-Allen, was published in London and New York in 1886. D'Arpentigny believed that there are six types of hands: elementary, spatulate, square, knotty, conic, and pointed or psychic. He later added a seventh category of "mixed" hands.

The Elementary Hand: Reflecting Earth Energy

The first category is known as the elementary hand (Figure 3.1). The purely elementary hand is an "earthy" hand, containing only a few basic lines.

The vast majority of people with elementary hands are male. They are often realistic, grounded in three-dimensional reality, and have the ability to function well in the material world. They tend to be deliberate, slow, and practical, and prefer to see things in a simple, uncomplicated way. This is not an indicator of low intelligence, but rather a particular view of the world.

For the most part, the owner of the elementary hand dislikes change, and prefers a stable and predictable work environment

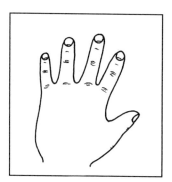

Figure 3.1: Elementary hand

with few, if any, surprises. Careers in agriculture, mining, work with heavy machinery, and similar activities involving strong physical labor are popular.

Elementary-handed people tend to be very attuned to nature, so they prefer to live and work in the country rather than in cities or towns. They work especially well with animals and plants. If you know people with the proverbial "green thumb," chances are good that they have elementary hands.

People with elementary hands have a tough physical

Appearance of the Elementary Hand

- Elementary hands are stiff and hard to the touch. They feel heavy and thick in their consistency.
- Palm tends to be broad and squarish.
- Fingers are short and stubby.
- Thumb is short, thick, and stiff; it will not bend backwards.
- The palm itself tends to be fleshy and usually contains very few lines; the three or four lines that appear tend to be strong and deep.
- Arch and loop fingerprints often predominate.
- Skin texture is coarse.

constitution and are often very strong. They can also be conservative and set in their ways. Steady and reliable, they like to be independent and their values are often material ones. When threatened, they can be violent. The purely elementary type is primitive, basic, crude, and unrefined. Intelligent reasoning and in-depth understanding may be lacking. People with elementary hands are often slow to react and are not likely to easily reveal their feelings, especially those of vulnerability and affection.

However, a "higher" elementary type (the type of person you are more likely to meet) may still have the characteristic shape of the elementary hand, but the consistency of the hand is more elastic and the skin may have a finer texture. This would reveal a more sensitive and flexible person, who is more receptive to new ideas and feelings. The handprint shown in Figure 3.2 can be classified as a more refined type of elementary hand. It belongs to a highly skilled automobile mechanic.

The Square Hand: Practical and Level-headed

The second category in the realistic classification is the square hand type (Figure 3.3). Recognized by its apparent squareness in form with squared-off fingertips, it is the hand of the organizer and planner.

Owners of this hand love order, method, and stability.

Figure 3.2: Print of higher elementary hand

Common sense rules their emotions, and they have a steady, systematic approach to life. They don't like confusion, and often have difficulty adapting to new circumstances and situations, especially when the hand and/or thumb is rigid. They are often thorough, competent, and careful with money.

Often lacking in spontaneity, people with squarish

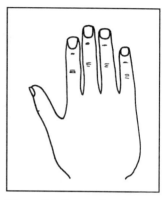

Figure 3.3: Square hand

APPEARANCE OF THE SQUARE HAND

- Squarish shape, with palm and fingers approximately the same length.
- Fingertips often squarish in form.
- Square nails, slightly longer than wide.
- Fingers and thumb are firm and do not easily bend outwards.
- Hand has a firm consistency.

hands prefer rules, methods, and structure. They believe in the "tried and true" and like to follow a fixed routine; and, unless the hand is flexible, they do not easily change.

People with squarish hands tend to be formal in their approach and are usually polite and reserved when dealing with others. They make excellent engineers, doctors, and bureaucrats. Square hands also give their owners an inordinate ability to persevere and to cope with difficult situations.

The Spatulate Hand: Action!

Spatulate hands (Figure 3.4) also fall into the realistic category. Their owners are often original and inventive, and are known for their restless and exploring personality.

The best word to describe this hand is *action*. People with spatulate hands are energetic, tenacious, innovative, and self-confident. They are also independent, self-reliant, and curious about new ideas and unusual experiences. Like those with

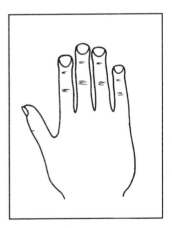

Figure 3.4: Spatulate hand

APPEARANCE OF THE SPATULATE HAND

- Hands are often broad and strong, with slightly knotted fingers.

- Fingertips "fan out" in the form of a spatula. The fingertip is often wider than the first phalange (the section at the base of the finger).

- Broad nails are common.

- The palm is wider at the knuckles than at the wrist.

square hands, they are often very practical and grounded in day-to-day reality.

People with spatulate hands tend to be creative and impulsive. They are generally extroverted, dynamic, and exciting to be with. They often have an uncanny ability to take advantage of a situation and use it to practical advantage.

Like those with elementary hands, owners of spatulate hands are sensual and favor activities on the material plane. Commerce, banking, construction, and entrepreneurship are popular career interests for them. They are also good inventors and athletes. When flexible and pliable, however, a spatulate hand increases an interest in sensual pleasures at the expense of work and other responsibilities.

The Conic Hand: Lover of Beauty

Unlike the previous hand types, conic or *artistic* hands (Figure 3.5) are of the receptive category. They belong to people who are emotional, intuitive, and changeable. This type of hand is especially common among women.

People with conic hands are governed by impulse and

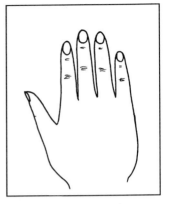

Figure 3.5: Conic hand

APPEARANCE OF THE CONIC HAND

- Conic hands tend to be slightly tapered at the base of the palm and at the tips of the fingers.

- The skin texture is usually fine, denoting sensitivity and a love of beauty.

- Soft yet springy consistency; flexible thumbs and fingers.

- In addition to the four major lines on the hand, there are usually a great number of fine lines, including lots of vertical lines.

first impressions. Unlike those with squarish hands, who are ruled by reason, conic-handed people are sentimental, intuitive, impulsive, capricious, and romantic.

Consistency is said to be a major problem for those who possess conic hands. They often begin a project with great enthusiasm and then leave it for someone else to complete, especially if the hands are flexible. Although they tend to support the efforts of others, they shift loyalties often and have difficulty with commitment.

Creativity is high. If the hand is firm and the lines well formed, creative energies are channeled towards mostly intellectual pursuits. When the hand is bland and fat, there is a strong sensuous nature. Rich foods, money, abundant sex, and comfortable surroundings are counted among their primary needs.

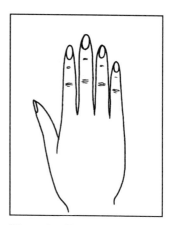

Figure 3.6: Psychic hand

The Psychic Hand: Painfully Idealistic

The psychic or *intuitive* hand (Figure 3.6) is relatively rare, but quite distinctive. It

APPEARANCE OF THE PSYCHIC HAND

- Hand is beautifully formed, and features long, graceful fingers with pointed tips.
- Consistency is soft and yielding.
- Flexible thumb and fingers.
- Very fine skin texture.
- Palm tends to have many lines.
- Nails tend to be oval, narrow, and quite long; when seen from the back, lots of skin is visible along the borders of the nail.

is essentially an extreme version of the conic hand.

Like people with conic hands, the owners of psychic hands are very sensitive and have a strong interest in beauty. There is also a tendency to be high-strung and impressionable, and many people with this type of hand have strong psychic ability.

People with psychic hands are motivated by their deepest feelings. They are highly creative and possess a strong imagination. Common sense is not one of their primary attributes, and they often have trouble dealing with the "nuts and bolts" of life.

Being grounded in the material world is an important

need for people with psychic hands. While they need to deepen their love of beauty and their innate interest in spiritual matters, they also need to learn how to function in the everyday world. For that reason, strong and steady friends are needed to help them deal with life's practical matters.

The Mixed Hand

Very few hands actually conform to any of the previous hand types in their pure form, although one type may predominate. For this reason, we have a fifth classification—the mixed hand—which can provide an important frame of reference.

By definition, the mixed hand (Figure 3.7) contains aspects found in one or more of the previous hand types. The hand may be primarily squarish, yet one or two fingers may be spatulate in shape. The overall shape of the hand may be conic, yet it also may contain elements found in the more practical square hand.

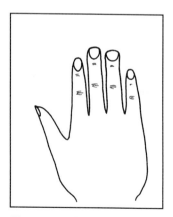

Figure 3.7: Mixed hand

The basic shape of the hand serves as the foundation of a careful hand analysis. The fingers, mounts, and lines, as well as modifiers like hand consistency and size, skin texture, flexibility, and skin ridge patterns, provide more specific information.

For these reasons, we need to take *all* factors into account when we study a hand, and evaluate the *relationships* among them. You can accomplish this goal by cultivating intuition and patience. With some practice, you will be able to achieve a basic "gestalt" of the hand after a few minutes of careful observation.

4

CONSISTENCY, SIZE, AND SKIN TEXTURE

When most people look at hands, they go straight to the lines. However, other aspects of the hand provide important background information on energy, strength, and character.

Consistency

Consistency is determined by measuring the hands' hardness or softness under pressure. Understanding the basic consistency of the hand helps us to determine both the person's energy level and how it is expressed in daily life. By taking your friend's hands in yours and gently squeezing them, you can gain an accurate idea about their consistency.

- With a *flabby hand*, the flesh easily crushes together when you squeeze gently. Such a hand reveals low physical energy, and as a result the individual has difficulty manifesting both feelings and concrete plans in the material world. In many cases, flabby hands are an indication of an idle, sensitive dreamer who dislikes both physical and emotional exertion.

- When the hands are *flabby and thick*, the sensual aspects of the personality are more pronounced. Over-indulgence in food, sex, drugs, or alcohol is common, and unless the thumb is strong, willpower is often absent.

- When the hands are *thin and weak*, the energy level of the individual tends to be low. People with such hands find it extremely difficult to sustain any long-term activity.

- *Soft hands* show a lack of bony feeling under pressure. Although soft hands can reveal a deficient energy level, there is far more potential for movement than in flabby hands. When the hands are soft and thick, earlier comments about overindulgence apply.

- *Elastic hands* cannot be easily crushed by your grasp, and tend to spring back under pressure. They show vitality, adaptability, and movement. In addition to strengthening the qualities revealed by the mounts, fingers, lines, and skin ridge patterns, they are found on people who like to invent and create. These people have an ability to respond easily to new ideas and adapt to unexpected circumstances.

- *Firm hands* are slightly elastic, and yield to moderate pressure. They reveal an energetic, active, and strong individual, who is both stable and responsible. While unable to adjust to new ideas and unexpected circumstances as easily as those with elastic hands, people with firm hands are able to take account of reality and adapt accordingly, even though such an effort may take time.

- *Hard hands* show no sign of yielding under pressure. Found mostly on men, these hands reveal no elasticity and are often coarse in texture. People with hard, rigid hands tend to be set in their ways. They lack mental flexibility and don't like change. Often they are prone to "hold in" their energy, which can result in sudden outbursts of temper and in stress-related diseases.

Flexibility

You can determine hand flexibility by the ease with which it bends backward. William G. Benham, in his classic text

The Laws of Scientific Hand Reading, wrote that the flexibility of the hand reveals "the degree of flexibility in the mind and nature, and the readiness with which this mind has power to unfold itself and 'see around the corner' of things."

- A *very flexible hand* can bend back to nearly a ninety-degree angle with a minimum of pressure. It reveals a person who is highly impressionable, easily ordered about by others, and who has difficulty in committing to one activity at a time. Such an individual frequently spends money faster than it is earned, and can be very unpredictable in both feelings and actions. If the thumb bends back easily as well, the person is generous to an extreme, and may easily be taken advantage of by others.

- A *moderately flexible hand* (Figure 4.1) bends back in a graceful arc. The owner of this type of hand can easily adapt to new and unforeseen

Figure 4.1: Moderately flexible hand

circumstances. The mind is versatile, intuitive, and impressionable. While it may be easy to feel, think, and act, there is nevertheless the danger of becoming involved in too many activities or projects at the same time.

- A *firm hand* hardly bends back at all under pressure. Although such a hand reveals an abundance of energy, there is a tendency to be careful with feelings, which are often kept hidden. While people with firm hands are open to new ideas, they are rarely impulsive and adapt to new circumstances and unfamiliar surroundings with difficulty.

- A *stiff hand* (Figure 4.2) is extremely rigid. While it reveals a person who is extremely cautious, highly responsible, and dedicated to hard work, the stiff hand betrays a rigid character structure. Its owners tend to be stubborn, set in their ways, and have difficulty dealing with new ideas and unexpected situations. People with stiff hands

Figure 4.2: Stiff hand

46

are often secretive and unwilling to share their personal problems or feelings with others.

Hand Size

The size of a person's hand is another indication of character. You need to determine it in the context of the person's overall size, including height, weight, and bone structure. Generally speaking, small hands reveal an individual who views life on a *grand scale*. While harboring a basic aversion to details and minutiae (unless their fingers are knotted), people with small hands tend to perceive the totality of what interests them, be it a flower, a creative project, or a scientific theory.

By contrast, people with *large hands* appear to gravitate more towards small things. While a woman with small hands would admire a large building in its entirety, her large-handed companion would probably focus her attention on the brass plaque by the main entrance. Large hands are often found on watchmakers, mathematicians, computer programmers, and others who are drawn to detailed work.

Unlike the apparently contradictory aspects of large and small hands, narrow and broad hands reveal corresponding aspects of the personality.

Narrow hands reveal a narrow, restricted way of looking at life, which is accentuated if the hands are also stiff and hard.

Conversely, *broad hands* are found on people who are broad-minded, tolerant, and interested in new concepts and trends.

Skin Texture

Aspects of skin texture also correspond with their emotional counterparts. The softer and finer the skin, the greater the degree of physical and emotional sensitivity.

- People with fine skin (Figure 4.3) are very sensitive to their surroundings and require an environment conducive to peace and harmony.

- Coarse skin texture (Figure 4.4) reveals a more rough-and-tumble individual, who is not strongly

Figure 4.3: Fine skin texture   Figure 4.4: Coarse skin texture

influenced by his or her emotional or physical surroundings.

Right or Left?

When we examine a person's hands, we need to discover
which of the two is dominant. The non-dominant or *passive*
hand reflects our past and our innate potential, while the
dominant or *active* hand shows primarily what we are doing
with our life at the moment. Very often the hands reveal
marked differences between our innate potential and the
degree to which it is being fulfilled.

Generally speaking, the dominant hand is the one we
write with. In the rare instances where an individual is
ambidextrous and writes with both hands, we need to
observe both hands together. When the hands are different,
we should ask questions as we proceed with the reading in
order to discover which of the two hands is dominant.

5

MOUNTS AND VALLEYS

The topography of the hand can be compared to the mountains, valleys, and plains of the Earth. The regions and mounts have much to tell us about our personality traits, innate talents, and energy level.

The hand is divided into six primary zones and then into eight mounts ("thenar elevations"), very much like the division of a geographic region into counties and towns. The zones provide a general orientation regarding latent capacities and outward expression, while the mounts reveal far more specialized information.

The Longitudinal Zones

The three longitudinal zones are formed by drawing an imaginary vertical line from a point between the index and middle fingers downwards towards the wrist and another to the wrist from a point between the middle and ring fingers (Figure 5.1).

- The first division forms the *active conscious zone*, which represents the energy we consciously apply in our dealings with the material world. It relates to the way we assert our ego in daily life both on an intellectual and concrete level. It is the region of practical knowledge, outward movement, and the application of principles in our work, study, and relationships.

- The zone located on the opposite third of the hand represents our hidden energy reserve, or the *passive subconscious zone*. It relates more to our innate creativity, emotional awareness, and instinctual capacity.

Figure 5.1: The longitudinal zones of the hand

- The middle zone, or *zone of balance*, serves as a meeting place in which these different energies can blend. This is an area in which we often find the line of Saturn (the line of life task), which moves up from the base of the palm towards the middle finger. It speaks of career, movement in life, and the degree to which we have found our life task or niche in the world.

The Latitudinal Zones

The three latitudinal zones (Figure 5.2) are formed by drawing a horizontal line from the tip of the thumb across to a point below the base of the fingers, and another from

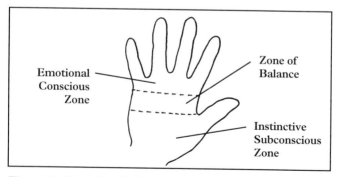

Figure 5.2: The latitudinal zones of the hand

just above the thumb ball directly across the palm.

- The first division, or the *emotional/conscious zone*, represents our active link with the world around us. Depending on the mounts that lie within it, it is the zone of emotional expression, the application of power, inspiration, ambition, artistic creation, and business acumen. It is the area of the hand that has kept the keenest sense of touch and holds the strongest power of connection with objects and people.

- The lower region or *instinctive subconscious zone*, is the zone of the Freudian "id" and our primary motivating forces. Depending on the mounts that lie within it, this zone relates to intuition, imagination, libido, and our deepest, most hidden desires.

- The middle horizontal zone is the practical *zone of balance*. It is the region of logic, common sense, and reason, and represents the blending of thought and feeling. It is the area that filters and absorbs our subconscious drives and helps guide them towards concrete expression. It integrates our aspirations and intellectual abilities with our physical and instinctual drives.

The Mounts

Each of the mounts (Figure 5.3) has a name, and characterizes the type of energy that is channeled through that

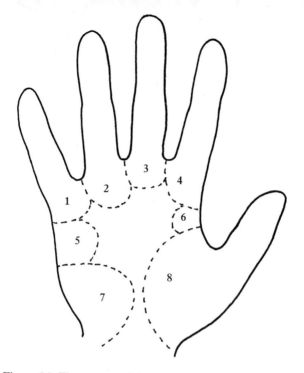

Figure 5.3: The mounts of the hand

1-Mercury
2-Apollo
3-Saturn

4-Jupiter
5-Upper Mars
6-Lower Mars

7-Luna
8-Venus

part of the hand. Mounts are named after planets, which are, in turn, named after Greek and Roman gods and goddesses. They represent aspects of our character that are symbolized by those mythological beings.

The strength of a particular mount depends on its size when compared with the other mounts of the hand. The more directly the mount is centered under the corresponding finger, the greater its strength and influence on the personality. You can determine the displacement of the mount by locating its *apex*. The apex of the mount is found where the ridges of the skin meet to form a pattern (Figure 5.4). If the apex of the Saturn mount, for example, is located more towards the mount of Apollo, it will take on some of the characteristics of the Apollo mount.

Remember that the strength of a particular mount can be modified by other aspects of the hand, such as the strength and shape of the corresponding finger as well as the clarity and strength of both major and minor lines.

Will

Logic

Mount
of Venus

Figure 5.4: The apex of the mount

The Mount of Jupiter

The mount of Jupiter is located beneath the index finger, and is named after Jupiter or Zeus, the king of the gods. This mount reflects the outgoing aspects: generosity, gregariousness, charisma, inspiration, and magnanimity. The mount of Jupiter also reveals our degree of self-confidence, leadership ability, executive skills, ambition, and spiritual inspiration.

- When the Jupiter mount is in a harmonious balance with the other mounts, you find healthy self assertion, a positive outlook, idealism, and the desire to move out towards others and help them.

- If the mount is unusually prominent, ambition plays a major role in the person's life. Egotism, vanity, and pride are strong, along with a tendency to be domineering and overbearing. If complemented by the fingers and lines, strong leadership and executive skills are indicated.

- When modified by other aspects of the hand, positive Jupiter traits can be distorted, and lead to a potential for greed, selfishness, arrogance, and lust for power and control.

- If this mount is deficient or flat, the individual is likely to have a poor self-image. Unless modified by other aspects, there is a lack of ambition and the drive to succeed. Such a person often feels awkward socially and has difficulty taking advantage of new opportunities.

The Mount of Saturn

The mount of Saturn, named after the god Saturn, "the judge," is found under the middle finger. While Jupiter represents the outgoing aspects of life, Saturn reflects the inward, self-directed side of the personality. When viewed in its positive light, it symbolizes introspection, responsibility, study, healthy self-preservation, and the inner search for truth. As a balancing force in the human personality, it enables us to sift through life's often conflicting currents, influences, and desires so that we can deal with them in a rational way.

- A normal mount of Saturn reveals a lover of independence and solitude who is able to balance the desire to be alone with the need to share the company of others. Fidelity, constancy, self-awareness, prudence, and emotional balance are found, along with the ability to study and explore new ideas.

- A highly developed Saturn mount often accentuates and distorts Saturn's essential qualities, especially if emphasized by other factors. Prudence can yield to fearful withdrawal, and healthy introspection can be overtaken by a tendency to be overly analytical and too self-absorbed. A strong mount can be found on many people who are rigid, taciturn, and defensive by nature.

The Mount of Apollo

Apollo is the god of power and self-expression, and his mount is located under the ring finger.

- A medium-sized mount of Apollo reveals a deep love of beauty and strong creative ability. This creative ability need not be restricted to art or music, but can include cooking, acting, writing, and design. If a person has an attractive home or dresses well, chances are that he or she has a well-developed mount of Apollo.

- Like the mounts of Jupiter and Saturn, a very large mount of Apollo can both strengthen and distort its basic "core" qualities. A preoccupation with pleasure, wealth, or fame are often revealed by a very prominent Apollo mount. A strong love of beauty can become a devotion to appearances and living on the periphery. Vanity and self-indulgence can replace the natural desire to look after our appearance and take good care of ourselves.

- When this mount is weak, the individual is lacking in

the essential Apollonian qualities. Instead of being exciting and filled with beauty, the person's life is ascetic, boring, and "flat." Deficiency in this mount can also indicate low physical energy.

The Mount of Mercury

Mercury was the messenger of the gods. For this reason, the mount of Mercury, located under the little finger, rules communication. It is the mount of spoken and written words, writing, healing, mathematics, commerce, and diplomacy. Mercury also governs wisdom and the ability to judge human nature.

- A well-developed mount of Mercury—especially when accompanied by a long finger—points towards commercial talent and oratorical skill. Actors, diplomats, salespeople, and public speakers almost always possess a strong mount of Mercury.

- A very prominent mount has no negative aspects by itself, although its positive qualities can be modified by a poorly-formed Mercury finger.

- A small, flat mount of Mercury—especially if accompanied by a short or weak finger—reveals a lack of commercial and scientific ability. Communication with others on a one-to-one basis may also be a problem, especially in close relationships.

The Mounts of Mars

There are two mounts of Mars (Fig. 5.3). Both reflect the qualities of the god of war, representing the dynamic, egotistical, and separative aspects of the personality. They speak of the desire to survive, to move forward, and to overcome obstacles and difficulties.

The *upper mount of Mars* (also known as "Mars negative") is located just under the mount of Mercury, and symbolizes determination and resistance.

- When well-formed and hard to the touch, it reflects a person who is both courageous and stubborn, and who resists being used or manipulated by others.

- A small or soft mount reveals a lack of valor and resistance. When found on a soft and flexible hand, the person is easily pushed around and has difficulty standing up for his or her rights.

- When extremely large and hard, violence and brutality are major components of the character.

Unlike the upper mount of Mars, which symbolizes passive resistance, the *lower mount of Mars* (also known as "Mars positive") reveals the more active and outgoing Martian qualities. Found between the mounts of Jupiter and Venus, it often appears as a small elevated pad, or "tumor" located just inside the thumb joint.

- A well-developed mount indicates strong self-assertion and the courage to face life's challenges and overcome them. It is often found on the hands of people involved with law enforcement or the military, and those in careers involving courage and strong self-assertion, such as hospital emergency room personnel and social workers who work with gangs or in dangerous neighborhoods.

- When this mount is large, hard, and reddish, the person has a strong temper.

- When this large mount is accompanied by a large mount of Venus, there is also an abundance of sexual passion.

- A small or deficient mount indicates a basically quiet, passive, and introverted individual who rarely expresses anger with others.

The Mount of Venus

Named after the goddess of love, the mount of Venus is an indicator of our aesthetic nature as well as our ability to love.

Ideally, the mount of Venus comprises the thumb ball and is outlined by a widely sweeping life line. On most people, this mount takes up approximately one-third of the palm and at best is neither too hard, too bland, nor too heavily lined. A good Venus mount should be smooth and firm to the touch, higher than the other mounts in elevation, and slightly pink in color.

- A normal-sized mount of Venus reveals warmth, vitality, and energy. It shows *joie de vivre* and the ability to love and be loved. A well-formed Venus mount also strengthens the life line and reveals a strong capacity to resist disease.

- When the mount is excessively large in relation to the other mounts, there is an abundance of physical passion, with a sizable appetite for sex, food, and drink.

- When the mount is also hard, this passion can easily spill over into aggression and brutality, especially if the mount is reddish and the skin texture coarse.

- A small, flat, or weak Venus mount reveals a lack of vital energy and physical passion. The personality tends to be somewhat lymphatic and cold, especially if the life line cuts through the Venus mount. Very often a strong love affair can actually increase the size of this mount.

People with strong musical talent often have prominent lower joints on the mount of Venus. In palmistry, they are known as "the angles" (Figure 5.5), and you can often see them on the hands of musicians, songwriters, singers, and dancers.

Figure 5.5: The "angles"

The Mount of Luna

Located opposite the mount of Venus just above the wrist, the mount of Luna represents the source of the receptive, passive, and emotional aspects of the personality. It is the home of our subconscious impressions and unconscious drives, instincts, and imagination.

Ideally, this mount should be broad and lightly rounded. It points to an interest in religion and mysticism, and a desire to perceive more than meets the eye. The medium-sized lunar mount reveals a good imagination balanced by reality.

- The stronger and more prominent the mount, the greater the imagination and subconscious drives—especially if the head line slopes downwards towards its center. Intuition is enhanced, along with the potential for creation.

- A large mount of Luna can also reveal a strong desire to protect and nurture others, especially if accompanied by a series of short vertical lines known as "Samaritan lines" on the Mercury mount. Many of the most interesting people in literature, the arts, and science have well-developed mounts of Luna.

Figure 5.6: Small diagonal lines on Luna mount

- The presence of small diagonal lines (Figure 5.6) tends to reveal a heightened degree of intuition, while unusual

Figure 5.7: Unusual skin ridge patterns

skin ridge patterns (Figure 5.7), highlight the presence of strong creative and instinctual abilities.

- When this mount is deficient or lacking, the individual tends to be too realistic, unimaginative, and dull. Fantasy is of no interest and imagination is seen as an indulgence of fools.

6

THE FINGERS

While the mounts and the basic form of the hand provide the groundwork we need to help determine character, the fingers offer a wealth of more specific information concerning both the personality and self-expression. In some cases, the fingers can tell us more about a person than any other single aspect of the hand.

When studying the fingers, it is important to consider each finger first by itself and then as an integral part of the hand. In addition, we must understand the relationship of each finger to the others.

We can determine the finger's relative strength in the hand by opening the palm completely, with fingers held together. If the fingers tend to lean towards one in particular, that finger is the dominant finger of the hand and provides us with the keynote of the individual's character. Figure 6.1 shows a hand with a dominant Saturn influence, because all the other fingers (including a strong Jupiter finger) bend towards Saturn.

Flexibility

Like the hands, the degree of flexibility of the fingers provides important clues to the person's character and ability to adapt. Ideally, the fingers should arch gently backward, revealing a capacity to adapt easily to new ideas and situations. When the top phalange of the finger bends back as well, strong creative talent is present. When the tip of the Mercury or little finger bends back, for example, it is a sign of writing or public speaking ability.

Length and Width

The length of the fingers must be judged in relation to the length of the palm. A balance exists if the size of the middle finger is the same length as the palm.

- Generally speaking, short fingers (Figure 6.2) reveal people who are intuitive, impatient, impulsive, and able to quickly grasp the essential points of an issue or situation. They tend to see things on a large scale, be they philosophical concepts, projects to be under-

Figure 6.1: Hand showing a dominant Saturn influence

taken, or panoramic views of the countryside. Unless their fingers are knotted, they also tend to overlook details.

- Long fingers (Figure 6.3) indicate opposite qualities. Patience, love of detail and analysis are common traits of long-fingered people. They like to focus on the minutiae of daily life, and tend to relate to the world in a more intellectual (as opposed to intuitive) way. Long fingers often reflect an introspective nature, with the tendency to hold grudges and harbor resentment.

- People with thick, fleshy fingers are basically sensual, seeking luxury, comfort, sex, good food, and other pleasures.

Figure 6.2: Hand with short fingers

Figure 6.3: Hand with long fingers

- Thin fingers tend to reveal a more intellectual person who is often removed from the material, three-dimensional world.

Knuckles

- Smooth fingers (Figure 6.4) have an absence of developed joints, and their owners tend to be intuitive and impulsive. Often impatient with details, they have difficulty breaking down a problem into its component parts. Their decisions are based primarily on hunches rather than a careful analysis of the facts. Psychologically, they are often in touch with their feelings and find it relatively easy to express anger, love, or joy.

Figure 6.4: Hand with smooth fingers

- If the fingers are short and smooth, impulsiveness, impatience, and aversion to detail are strong.

- Long, smooth fingers will tend to strengthen the

intellectual and analytical aspects of the personality.

- Knotty fingers that are not due to arthritis (Figure 6.5) reveal a strong analytical mind. Their owners are rarely seduced by appearances and tend to penetrate deeply into an issue using logic, detail, and analysis.

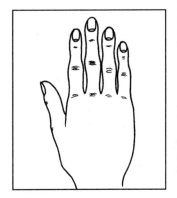

Figure 6.5: Hand with knotted fingers

Psychologically, people with knotty fingers tend to lack spontaneity and find it difficult to express their feelings directly.

The Phalanges

The index, middle, ring, and little fingers are divided into three parts or *phalanges*

Figure 6.6: The three phalanges of the fingers

71

(Figure 6.6). The top phalange is that of mental order; the middle phalange is that of practical order; the bottom phalange is called the phalange of material order.

- When the top phalange is the longest of the three, thinking absorbs most of the person's attention.

- A long middle phalange shows that the primary keynote—as expressed by the particular finger's significance—is action.

- A long and thick phalange of a material order reveals that the person is more grounded in the material or instinctual aspects of life, like money, products, or people. A long, thick phalange at the base of the Jupiter finger is a sign of a materialist who is very much interested in accumulating money, people, and possessions. Many are also good business people. The length of the phalanges may vary from finger to finger.

Finger Types

Fingers come in five basic shapes, each one revealing a specific "core quality" of the personality. Since most hands have a number of finger shapes, look at the qualities governing each individual finger as well as the finger's basic form.

Squarish fingertips (Figure 6.7) reveal order and regularity. Perseverance, foresight, structure, and organization are strong. People with squarish fingertips have a capacity to exhibit rational, decisive action.

Spatulate fingertips (Figure 6.8) reveal an energetic, active, and impulsive person. Owners of spatulate fingers tend to be adventurous, self-confident, and down-to-earth in their approach to life.

Conic fingertips (Figure 6.9) show a receptive and sensitive nature. People with conic fingers tend to respond strongly to outer stimuli, and are governed by impulse and first impressions. Conic fingertips are often found on artistic people.

Figure 6.7: Squarish finger

Figure 6.8: Spatulate finger

Figure 6.9: Conic finger

Pointed or *psychic fingertips* (Figure 6.10) are somewhat rare. They reveal a strong tendency to be affected by the outer environment, and show a dreamy, intuitive, or inspirational type of mind.

Round fingertips (Figure 6.11) are the most common. They reveal an adaptable, well-rounded, and balanced personality—active yet receptive, mental yet emotional.

Many hands are a combination of these types. Remember to take into account the qualities governing each individual finger, as well as the finger's basic form.

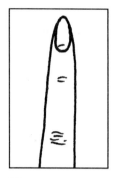

Figure 6.10:
Psychic finger

Fingerprints

Even if you are not wanted by the FBI, your fingerprints are important. They represent the most basic and unchangeable elements of your personality. Although you can learn to modify the traits they reflect, you can never be rid of them completely.

Figure 6.11: Round finger

Scientists have named these fine skin ridges *dermatoglyphics* (skin carvings).

Ridge lines in the skin run all over the palm of the hand, as well as the soles of the feet. Some form distinct patterns, such as loops and whorls.

Essentially, there are three basic types of fingerprints: the whorl, the arch, and the loop. They account for approximately eighty per cent of all fingerprint patterns.

Whorls

The *whorl* (Figure 6.12) is the sign of the individualist and the specialist. People whose fingerprints are mainly

---

POSITIVE QUALITIES OF THE WHORL INCLUDE

- independence
- love of freedom
- overall ability

NEGATIVE TRAITS ARE

- tendency towards isolation
- secretiveness
- self-obsession

---

of the whorl type will tend to be original thinkers with clearly formed opinions. They often seek to carve out their own niche in life and become experts in some specialized area.

When whorls predominate on the fingers, people can become a "law unto themselves," disregarding convention if it gets in the way of their personal desires. They also tend to dislike others interfering in their personal affairs. Whorls are often found on the hands of reformers as well as career criminals, because both defy social convention and are unhappy with the status quo.

Very often a predominance of whorls can indicate a special talent or ability that distinguishes the person from others.

Figure 6:12 Whorl fingerprint

Figure 6.13: Arch fingerprint

Arches

The *arch* (Figure 6.13) is a sign of capability and trustworthiness. People whose fingerprints are primarily of the arch pattern tend to be practical, hardworking, efficient, and good with their hands. They are often attracted to such professions as craftspeople, farmers, mechanics, and surgeons. They are frequently better able to express themselves through actions than words.

Generally speaking, the higher the arch, the more skillful and idealistic the individual.

POSITIVE QUALITIES OF THE ARCH INCLUDE

- steadiness
- realism
- usefulness

NEGATIVE TRAITS ARE

- emotional repression
- suspicious nature
- reluctance to accept change
- difficulty in responding to new ideas or unexpected situations

---

Loops

The *loop* (Figure 6.14) is by far the most common fingerprint pattern. It represents an easy-going, adaptable, middle-of-the-road personality. Owners of hands where loops predominate are generally easy to get along with, and able to adapt easily to new and varied social situations. They are also able to tune in to different intellectual concepts with little difficulty,

Figure 6.14: Loop fingerprint

POSITIVE QUALITIES OF THE LOOP INCLUDE

- flexible personality
- ability to have a well-rounded view of things

NEGATIVE TRAIT

- the tendency to lack individuality. Wherever a loop is found, it reveals basic "middle ground" tendencies in the area that the particular finger represents.

---

and react quickly to changing social situations, especially if their hands are flexible as well.

Other Fingertip Patterns

There are also three less common fingerprint patterns:

The *tented arch* (Figure 6.15) earns its name from a vertical line in the middle that looks like a tent-pole. Although it still reflects the qualities of the ordinary arch, it is a sign of a heightened degree of emotional sensitivity, idealism, and enthusiasm.

Figure 6.15: Tented arch fingerprint

The *high loop* (Figure 6.16) looks like the normal loop pattern, except that it reaches higher up on the fingertip than a regular loop. It reveals high intelligence and an optimistic personality.

The *composite* pattern is also known as the "double loop" or "twinned loop." It is composed of two loops curling around each other (Figure 6.17). It is a sign of duality—a natural ability to see both sides of any issue. This print is often

Figure 6.16: High loop finger-print

Figure 6.17: Composite fingerprint

found among mediators, analysts, therapists, lawyers, and counselors, where a look at all aspects of a situation is useful.

People with twinned loops, however, often have difficulty in making decisions for themselves; they want to find out all they can before they feel competent to make a decision. They may take forever to make a purchase in a store or change their job or relationship, especially if the lines of life and head are connected at their commencement.

Strong, clear fingerprint patterns intensify the meaning of each type and bring out its positive qualities. When, at times, we come across eccentric or strangely-formed prints, they invariably accompany strange or eccentric personalities.

The Thumb

In Hindu palmistry, the thumb is considered so important that many hand readers restrict themselves to studying the thumb alone when they analyze character.

The thumb relates to our ego strength and our level of energy or life force. Because it permits us to accomplish a wide variety of tasks in daily life, the thumb also symbolizes our ability to express this energy and power in the world.

The size of the thumb is an index to the basic energy level of the individual. Normally, the tip of the thumb reaches the lower phalange of the index (or Jupiter) finger. A long thumb (Figure 6.18), often called a "capable" thumb, indicates an abundance of energy in addition to a forceful personality.

Figure 6.18: Long thumb

Figure 6.19: Short thumb

Individuals with short thumbs (Figure 6.19) tend to be weak-willed and are seldom known for their strong character, especially if the thumb bends back easily under pressure. They often lack self-confidence, forcefulness, and the ability to follow through with a project or other endeavor.

However, before we proclaim a thumb to be long or short, we need to take account of how it is set on the hand. A *low-set thumb* is easy to position at a ninety degree angle to the index finger (Figure 6.20). It reveals a person who is adaptable, independent, and takes risks.

When the thumb is *set high* in the hand (Figure 6.21), the person tends to withhold energy. There is a fear of letting go and moving with the flow of life. He or she might be

Figure 6.20: Low-set thumb   **Figure 6.21: High-set thumb**

FINGERPRINT PATTERNS ON THE THUMB

- A whorl on the thumb reveals strong willpower and an individualistic way of doing things.
- An arch is a sure sign of a practical doer who has a commonsense approach to dealing with new projects or life challenges.
- A composite pattern reveals a tendency to examine all sides of an issue. It can also betray indecisiveness in approaching and executing projects, which means that they could take a long time to complete.
- A tented arch combines practicality with enthusiasm.
- A loop reveals average, middle-of-the-road qualities. It is by far the most common pattern found on the thumb.

---

described as "uptight," unless modifying aspects are present, such as overall flexibility and a separation between the life and head lines at their commencement.

The thumb is divided into three parts (Figure 6.22). The nail phalange is called the *phalange of will*, while the second is the *phalange of logic*. The third part of the thumb is the mount of Venus, discussed earlier (see pages 61–62).

The Phalange of Will

- A strong phalange of will—one that is well-rounded, long, and wide—indicates decisiveness, "staying power," and the ability to transform thoughts into deeds.

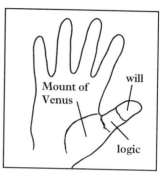

Figure 6.22: The three phalanges of the thumb

- When this phalange is conic in shape, there may be a lack of resistance; the person's energy tends to scatter when confronted with a major project or serious problem requiring long-term attention.

- If this phalange is thin or flat (viewed from the side), the person tends to be high-strung and nervous (Figure 6.23).

Figure 6.23: Flat thumbtip

- When the fingertip is squarish, there is an ability to organize and execute projects.

- A spatulate tip is the sign of dynamic individuals with a zest for living. Things "happen" around them.

Certain fingerprint patterns have a special meaning when found on the thumb.

Some people have a thumb with a deformed will phalange that has a bulbous or clubbed appearance. Palmists have called it a "Murderer's thumb" (Figure 6.24). While it does not necessarily indicate homicidal tendencies, it is often a sign of a person who tends to withhold energy to such an extent that strong, sudden bursts of temper can result. This holding back of energy may also result in physical or psychological problems, like high blood pressure and other stress-related diseases.

Figure 6.24: "Murderer's thumb"

The Phalange of Logic

The phalange of logic reveals our degree of reasoning power. Ideally, it should be the same length and strength as the will phalange, which would indicate a balance between thought and action.

- The longer and thicker the phalange, the more the ego will exert strong control over action. In extreme cases, constant reasoning can kill movement altogether. This is especially true if the thumb joint is knotted.

- A thick phalange has been interpreted by palmists to mean that the owner tends to be frank and blunt with others.

- A "waisted" phalange (Figure 6.25) is an indicator of tact and diplomacy. Some believe it means that logic is not a major component of the personality.

Figure 6.25: Waisted thumb

Flexibility

- A supple thumb (Figure 6.26) bends back at the joint, indicating emotional versatility and an ease in adapting. The person is generous, although careful.

- When the thumb is extremely flexible—bending back ninety degrees or more—the person can be generous to a fault and likely to be extravagant with money, especially if the rest of the hand is flexible as well. Will power tends to be poor.

Figure 6.26: Supple thumb

- A moderately flexible thumb bends back only slightly under pressure. It reveals a practical individual who relies on common sense. While it indicates a strong and determined will, there is nevertheless a degree of open-mindedness and the ability to adapt.

- A stiff thumb (Figure 6.27) will not bend back under pressure. Owners of stiff thumbs tend to be stubborn, prudent, and have tremendous difficulty adapting to new ideas and situations. On the more positive side, they are generally very stable and highly responsible. They can be relied upon for

Figure 6.27: Stiff thumb

almost anything. The qualities of a stiff thumb can be offset by a flexible hand.

The Jupiter Finger

Like its corresponding mount, the index or Jupiter finger represents leadership, ambition, and the drive to succeed in life. Ideally, it should be the same length as the ring (or Apollo) finger, and slightly shorter than the middle (or Saturn) finger.

- If the Jupiter finger is longer than the Apollo, the ego is strong, with a healthy amount of self-esteem. People with Jupiter fingers like to be in charge; they like to be the boss. Natural leaders, they are often involved in running a business, a school, or in some other job calling for executive or administrative ability. However, a long Jupiter finger (especially if it curves inward) can reveal a tendency to be vain, domineering, and controlling.

- To the degree that the Jupiter finger is shorter than Apollo, there is a corresponding lack of self-esteem and self-confidence. The person tends to underestimate his or her talents and accomplishments, especially if the head and life lines join together.

- To the extent that the Jupiter finger bends towards Saturn, the person tends to be insecure. This often

FINGERPRINT PATTERNS ON THE JUPITER FINGER

Fingerprints have different meanings on Jupiter.

- A loop fingerprint pattern has no special meaning.
- A whorl on the fingertip is a sign of individuality and original thinking.
- An arch reveals practical ability in dealing with both work and hobbies, as well as a talent for fixing or repairing machinery or other objects. It can also mean the ability to know how to "fix" a situation that isn't working.
- The presence of a tented arch is believed to increase one's general enthusiasm when dealing with personal goals and inner beliefs. It also reveals a strong social consciousness.
- A composite print indicates indecisiveness regarding life goals or beliefs. Because a composite print reveals the ability to clearly see both sides of an issue, it is often difficult to choose a specific course of action.

shows up in his or her life as jealousy, possessiveness, and acquisitiveness. People with bent index fingers can often be found browsing through shopping malls, antique shops, used book stores, and flea markets, looking for something to add to their particular collection.

- When this finger is conic or pointed, religious feelings are strong. Such fingers are often found on people who have the ability to inspire and motivate others, especially if the finger is long.

- A spatulate index fingertip adds a streak of dynamism to the personality.

- A squarish tip reveals executive or administrative ability.

The Saturn Finger

The middle finger is named for Saturn. It is the finger of propriety, responsibility, and introspection. It serves as a "balance finger" between the subconscious aspects of the personality, represented by Apollo and Mercury, and the more active, conscious qualities of the thumb and Jupiter finger.

- A long Saturn finger reaches high above the other fingers on either side. It reveals a person who treats life with the utmost seriousness. People involved with scientific research and business people who deal with large amounts of money tend to have long Saturn fingers.

- When the finger is unusually short (the same length or shorter than either the Jupiter or Apollo finger), the owner tends to be careless and does not like to take on responsibility. Most of us have a Saturn

Fingerprint Patterns on the Saturn Finger

- A whorl shows a current of individuality in the working life, which can lead the person to select an unusual career or unconventional line of work or hobby.

- An arch reveals a practical attitude towards investments and home improvements.

- A tented arch is believed to add enthusiasm when undertaking difficult projects.

- A composite pattern tends to reveal a sense of ambivalence towards one's career, and is often found on people who are endlessly searching for "the right job."

finger that is neither abnormally long nor short.

- When straight, there is a harmonious relationship between will and emotion, as well as a balance between liking to be with people and wanting to be alone.

- When Saturn curves slightly towards Jupiter, the person tends to be generally spontaneous and outgoing, enjoying being in the company of others as much as possible.

- A slight curve towards Apollo indicates a need to be alone more than not.

- A prominent curve or bend towards Apollo (that is not the result of arthritis or accident) can indicate chronic melancholy or depression. When you observe such a formation, take special care to look for confirming or modifying aspects in the rest of the hand, particularly on the head line.

The Apollo Finger

Like its corresponding mount, the ring or Apollo finger rules creativity, the love of art and music, and the ability to express ourselves, especially in the public arena.

- A long, straight Apollo finger is found on many artists, actors, dancers, and others who work primarily with the public.

- When the finger features a spatulate tip, the ability to work with the public is enhanced. It is often found on public speakers, teachers, actors, and singers.

- A conic tip reveals a strong artistic sensibility as well as a good sense of style.

- Straight Apollo fingers indicate an ability to judge others quickly and accurately.

- A ring finger that bends slightly towards Saturn betrays a tendency to overestimate others. This often results in disillusion when they don't live up to our high standards.

- According to some hand readers, an Apollo finger that bends sharply towards Saturn is a sure indication of a gambler and libertine.

FINGERPRINT PATTERNS ON THE APOLLO FINGER

Fingerprint patterns modify the meaning of this finger:

- Loop reveals a "middle of the road" aspect to the personality and has no special meaning.

- A whorl fingertip pattern on Apollo is a sign of strong artistic skills, and is often found on the hands of painters, graphic artists, and designers.

- An arch pattern indicates a more sensual creative application, and is found more on sculptors, woodworkers, and metalworkers.

- A tented arch reveals special enthusiasm for a particular form of art.

- A composite pattern indicates variable taste in art. People with composite prints on Apollo often make continual changes in their way of dressing or in their home decor.

The Mercury Finger

The little finger or Mercury finger rules communication, and the longer the finger, the greater the ability to communicate with others. Ideally, this finger should reach to the top phalange of Apollo. In some cases, it is set low on the palm, which makes it appear shorter than it really is. If this is the case, place the Mercury finger over the Apollo finger of the other hand to determine its actual length.

- A high percentage of successful public speakers, evangelists, actors, writers, dancers, politicians, salespeople, lawyers, and business people have long, well-developed Mercury fingers. Some palmists believe that a long Mercury finger is also the sign of a good lover, because such an individual can communicate on an intimate level as well as in the public arena.

- A short little finger can indicate difficulty in relating to other people, both publicly and privately. When this finger is short, it is not easy making oneself understood, and close relationships are often difficult to establish and maintain.

- A straight Mercury finger indicates honesty, frankness, and trustworthiness.

- A slight curving towards Apollo reveals a degree of astuteness and diplomacy.

FINGERPRINT PATTERNS ON THE MERCURY FINGER

The Mercury finger nearly always has a loop finger-print pattern, unless all the other fingerprints on the hand are of another type.

- A whorl on Mercury alone shows a special talent in verbal or written expression.
- An isolated arch on this finger is too rare to make a general interpretation.

- A sharp bending towards Apollo (not the result of arthritis or accident) indicates a tendency to be manipulative and even dishonest. When the hand features a sharply bending Jupiter finger as well, the individual would stop at nothing to obtain what he or she wants.

Finger Spacing

When the fingers are held closely together on an open hand, the individual tends to be somewhat contracted and fearful, lacking self-confidence and independence. The wider the spacing between the fingers, the greater the open-ness, independence, and daring.

- When the Jupiter finger breaks away from the rest of the hand, leadership and self-reliance are increased. Very often, a shy, insecure person with a short index finger attempts to overcome these problems by becoming overly aggressive and independent, and that will show up here. People with this feature enjoy being the center of attention. It is also a sure sign of a liking to be self-employed, or at least to have a good degree of independence at work.

- To the degree that the space between the Apollo and Mercury fingers is wide, the person is an independent, unconventional thinker. Because such an individual does not conform to the expectations of society, sexual or emotional problems may be evident.

Nails and Personality

Although the fingernails are most useful in medical diagnosis, they can also help us evaluate character. Ideally, the nails should be slightly longer than wide, and slightly curved as opposed to flat (Figure 6.28).

Figure 6.28: Normal nail

- People with long nails are often drawn to artistic pursuits and like to think and analyze.

- Narrow nails reveal a narrow, dogmatic outlook on life and little openess to new ideas and trends.

- Broad nails reveal a broad-minded personality.

- Short nails (that are not the result of nail biting) indicate an impatient and often critical personality.

See more about nails in Chapter 10.

7

THE LINES

The lines of the hand can be compared to the interstates, highways, and country lanes of a road map. They indicate our major talents and energies, our capacity to manifest these talents in life, and the probable directions these talents and energies will take us. In essence, the lines of the hand form a natural map of our life course, while allowing for occasional detours and changes in direction according to our free will.

The lines of the hand (known scientifically as *flexion creases*) not only reveal the past and the present, but also provide important insights into the future. The major lines of the hand are shown in Figure 7.1.

We do not fully understand how the lines are formed. Some feel that they are "rivers of energy" that come through the fingers and into the palm. Others claim that

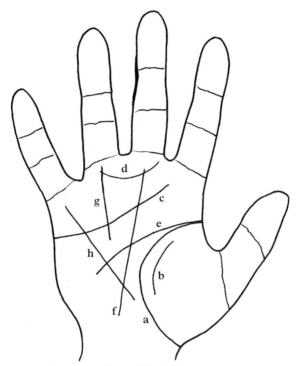

Figure 7.1: The major lines of the hand

a-Life	d-Girdle of Venus	g-Apollo
b-Inner Life	e-Head	h-Mercury
c-Heart	f-Saturn	

the lines are affected by messages from the brain to the nerves, which are connected to the skin of the hand. We know that along with skin ridge patterns (such as fingerprints), the three major lines of the hand (life, head, and heart) first appear within several months after conception, and are subject to genetic influences and the foetus' environment in the womb. However, unlike skin ridge patterns that stay the same, the lines in the hand often change gradually throughout our lifetime. We also know that the form and number of lines are not dependent on hand movements, nor on what we do for a living. However, sedentary individuals often have more lines than those who perform heavy manual labor.

In some cases, the lines of the hand can change in a matter of weeks, although most changes can be seen every few years. They are affected by the introduction of "stressors" in life (such as exposure to a dangerous virus or drug abuse), as well as by attitude modification and changes in personal behavior. Learning how to meditate, cutting down on cigarettes, or devoting more time and energy to making a relationship work can alter the lines of the hand dramatically.

If you're interested in achieving your full potential, the objective knowledge offered by the ever-changing lines can be both valuable and exciting. The lines show that we are indeed the "master of our fate" and can assume personal responsibility for our life and its direction.

Line Quality and Quantity

Ideally, lines should be clear and well-defined.

- The line's depth and width should be even. A particularly deep line reveals excessive energy, while a broad, shallow line indicates a lack of strength and focus. Generally speaking, the stronger the line, the stronger its influence.

- The number of lines on the hand is also important. An abundance of lines (Figure 7.2) indicates hypersensitivity and nervousness. It can also show that the individual has many paths through which to express his or her talents.

- Having few lines on the hand (Figure 7.3) generally indicates little sensitivity with few basic channels for life expression.

Before we go into detail about each of the lines, there are several important formations we need to be familiar with.

- *Splintering* or *splitting* of a line (Figure 7.4) dissipates its strength and focus. In some cases, a split indicates a change or a new phase in a person's life, so its existence is not necessarily a negative sign.

- *Lines of influence* (Figure 7.5) are small lines that cross or run parallel to the major lines. We'll discuss them later.

Figure 7.2: Hand showing an abundance of lines

Figure 7.3: Hand showing few lines

Figure 7.4: Splintering or splitting of a line

Figure 7.5: Lines of influence

- *Islands* (Figure 7.6) form where there is a splitting of a line that reunites later on. Islands impair the line's strength and indicate a lack of focus and dissipation of energy.

- A *chain* (Figure 7.7) is composed of many islands together, and indicates a prolonged period of vacillation and scattered energy. The line is weakened as a result.

- A *fork* (Figure 7.8) appears at the end of a line where the line splits. Depending on its location, it can indicate either a dissipation of the basic energies represented in the line, or balance and adaptability.

Figure 7.6: Islands

Figure 7.7: A chained line

Figure 7.8: A forked line

- A *dot* (Figure 7.9) appears as a slight colored indentation on the line. The existence of a dot indicates a physical or emotional setback of some kind, depending on its color and location.

- A *grille* (Figure 7.10) is formed by numerous fine lines that crisscross. It generally indicates a

Figure 7.9: A dotted line

Figure 7.10: Lines forming a grille

period of diffused and scattered energy.

- A *square* (Figure 7.11) is formed by four independent lines that create a rectangle. It is a sign of protection and preservation and often repairs a broken line.

Figure 7.11: Lines forming a square

The Life Line

The life line (*thenar crease*) is the principal line of the hand (Figure 7.1a). It begins at the edge of the palm between the thumb and forefinger, and arcs downwards around the mount of Venus. It is the primary indicator of the strength of our physical constitution and our level of vital force. This line records periods of disease, accident, and other major events. It also indicates the possible length of time we will live. Figure 7.12 shows how to estimate time on the life line and on other major lines of the hand.

When attempting to determine the length of life, three basic factors need to be taken into account.

- When the life line is the same length on both hands, the ending of the line indicates the possible time of death.

- If the lines are of different lengths, the line on the active hand is more likely to be correct.

- A long head, heart, and/or career line can modify a short life line, just as an abrupt termination of one or more of these lines can indicate a shorter life span.

Never predict a time of death. In the first place, there is a good chance you will be wrong. Many people with short life lines have been known to live to become great-grandparents, while others with long life lines have been known to die at a relatively young age. Also, by predicting the time of death you

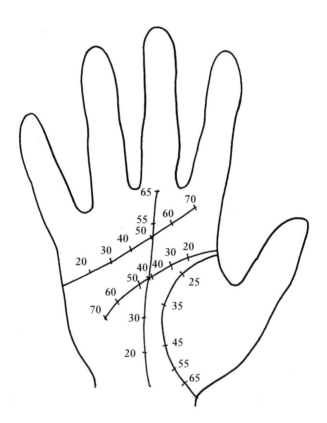

Figure 7.12: Estimating time on the major lines of the hand

may be planting a "seed thought" in the person's mind, which can have unfortunate, self-fulfilling results.

Whenever you see a short or broken life line, be sure to mention that the lines of the hands are not set in concrete, and that they can change according to our attitudes and habits. The life line is one of the most responsive to changes in attitude and lifestyle.

No two life lines are the same, although most conform to some of the following brief descriptions:

- *Long, clear, and well-marked* (Figure 7.13): Strong physical constitution, good health, vitality, resistance to disease, ability to meet life's challenges, probable long life.

- *Short, clear and well-marked* (Figure 7.14): Intensity, good health, possible short life. See other lines for modifying factors.

- *Red and deep*: Powerful energy, intensity, aggressive or violent disposition. Observe other hand characteristics for possible modifying factors.

Figure 7.13: Long, clear and well-marked life line

- *Wide, not well-marked:* Personality is easily influenced by outside stimuli.

- *Long and weak* (Figure 7.15): Weak constitution, vulnerability to disease, tendency towards nervousness and indecision.

- *Islands* (Figure 7.16): Lapses in health or general physical weakness. Obstacles, periods of indecision, or lack of focus.

- *Breaks* (Figure 7.17): Interruptions in the tenor of life, either physical, psychological, or both.

- *Separated from head line* (Figure 7.18): Impulsive, impatient, self-reliant, extroverted. Can be reckless.

Figure 7.14: Short, clear and well-marked life line

Figure 7.15: Long and weak life line

Figure 7.16: Islands on the life line

Figure 7.17: Breaks in the life line

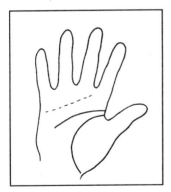

Figure 7.18: Life line separated from head line

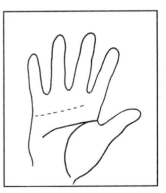

Figure 7.19: Life line connected to head line

- *Connected to head line* (Figure 7.19): Careful and cautious, takes a long time to make decisions. The point where the lines separate indicates the age of independence from the family physically and/or psychologically. In general, the longer the lines are connected, the longer it takes to make decisions and act independently.

- *Forming broad arc around Venus mount* (Figure 7.20): Warm, sensual, emotionally responsive.

- *Hugging close to thumb, cutting into Venus mount* (Figure 7.21): Inhibited, cold, unresponsive.

- *Moving towards mount of Luna* (Figure 7.22): Naturally restless. Love of travel and change of scene.

Figure 7.20: Life line forming broad arc around Venus mount

Figure 7.21: Life line hugging close to thumb, cutting into Venus mount

- *Branch from life line moving up towards Jupiter finger* (Figure 7.23): Optimism, ambition, drive to overcome obstacles.

More about the life line appears in Chapter 10.

The Inner Life Line

This line (known as a "sister line") provides added strength and protection to the life line (Figure 7.1b). It increases vital-

Figure 7.22: Life line moving towards mount of Luna

Figure 7.23: Branch from life line moving upwards towards Jupiter mount

113

ity and lends support (either physical or psychological) in the event of an accident, health problem, or other difficulty.

The Heart Line

The upper transverse crease or *heart line* (Figure 7.1c) is our emotional barometer. Moving from beneath the Mercury finger across the palm, it reveals the quality of our emotions, our degree of sensitivity, and our capacity for love and affection. This line can also provide important information regarding the physical condition of the heart as well as the strength and type of our sexual desire.

The ideal heart line (Figure 7.24) is smooth, of good color, and relatively free from islands and breaks. It curves upwards slightly and ends between the Saturn and Jupiter fingers, indicating a balance between the mind and emotions. Two or three small branches appear at its end, revealing a balance between sentiment, common sense, and physical passion.

Figure 7.24: The "ideal" heart line

- *A straight heart line* (Figure 7.25) reveals a more mental type of lover. Fantasies, images, and romance are important aspects of a sexuality that is primarily receptive in nature.

- *When the line curves upwards* (Figure 7.26), a more physical or instinctual sexuality predominates. Sexual expression will probably be more active and assertive.

- *Ending under Saturn* (Figure 7.27): Predominantly a physical type of sexuality; run more by the head than the heart in love relationships; can be emotionally cut off; strong sexual instincts.

Figure 7.25: A straight, "mental" heart line

Figure 7.26: Heart line curving upwards

Figure 7.27: Heart line ending under Saturn

Figure 7.28: Heart line ending between Saturn and Jupiter

- *Ending between Saturn and Jupiter* (Figure 7.28): Balance between reason and emotion; warm-hearted, generous, sympathetic.

- *Ending under Jupiter* (Figure 7.29): Idealistic; ruled more by the heart than the head in relationships; mental and emotional

Figure 7.29: Heart line ending under Jupiter

type of sex urges; a romantic, devotional, poetic type of love.

- *Dropping to life and head lines* (Figure 7.30): Strong conflicts between the heart and the head; powerful emotions; easier to love "humanity" than individuals.

- *Chained heart line* (Figure 7.30a): High degree of sensitivity; easily hurt and affected by others. Desire for intimate contact, with accompanying fear of commitment. Tendency to fall in and out of love frequently.

- *Branches at the end of the heart line* (Figure 7.31): Receptive nature.

Figure 7.30: Heart line dropping to the head and life lines

Figure 7.30a: Chained heart line

- *Dots*: Possible heart disease. (See Chapter 10.)

- *Line joining heart line with head line*: (Figure 7.32): Balance between emotions and intellect in relationships.

- *Wide space between lines of heart and head* (Figure 7.33): Broad-minded, unconven-

Figure 7:31: Branches at the end of the heart line

Figure 7.32: Line joining heart line with head line

Figure 7.33: Wide space between lines of heart and head

118

tional outlook. Impulsive and impatient, especially if life and head lines are separate.

- *Narrow space between heart and head lines* (Figure 7.34): Tendency to be narrow-minded and secretive. Repressed personality.

Figure 7.34: Narrow space between heart and head lines

The Girdle of Venus

The Girdle of Venus (Figure 7.1d) is like a second heart line, located between the heart line and the top of the palm. Found on perhaps ten per cent of the population, its presence indicates sensitivity and emotional responsiveness. The more clear and well-defined, the more balanced and properly channeled these emotions will be. For an excellent example of a well-formed girdle, see Figure 7.35 and also Figure 11.7 on page 229.

Altruism, compassion, and sexual responsiveness are strong attributes of a Girdle of Venus. However, if the girdle is broken and poorly defined (Figure 7.36) the person may be promiscuous, moody, and self-indulgent. Examine the entire hand before arriving at such conclusions.

Figure 7.35: A well-formed Girdle of Venus

Figure 7.36: Broken and poorly formed Girdle of Venus

The Head Line

The lower transverse crease or *head line* starts at the beginning of the line of life and moves horizontally across the hand (Figure 7.1e). It reveals our intelligence, our way of thinking and our psychological disposition. The head line also records periods of emotional difficulty, mental illness, and any accidents or illnesses that affect the head.

A "good" head line is long, clear, and free of islands,

dots, and breaks. It should slope gently downward and end with a small fork, denoting a balance between realism and imagination. This feature is often found on the hands of writers, and is known in palmistry as the "writer's fork."

- *Long* (Figure 7.37): Intelligence, mental and emotional flexibility, wide range of intellectual interests.

- *Short, just reaching the Saturn finger* (Figure 7.38): Thought processes are limited primarily to mundane affairs.

- *Strong* (Figure 7.39): Good mental powers and focus. Ability to concentrate.

- *Weak* (Figure 7.40): Scattered intellect. Emotional

Figure 7.37: Long head line   Figure 7.38: Short head line

difficulties, poor concentration.

- *Islanded* (Figure 7.41): Difficulty in concentration. Worry; psychological disturbances.
- *Wavy* (Figure 7.42): Vacillation.
- *Moving straight across the hand* (Figure 7.43): Practical, realistic, analytical.
- *Sloping slightly downwards towards Luna mount* (Figure 7.44): Good imagination, creative intellect.
- *Sloping strongly towards Luna mount* (Figure 7.45): Very strong and fertile imagination; tendency to live in a dream world. If line is broken, possible suicidal fantasies.

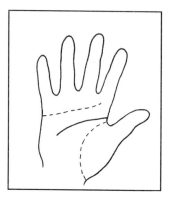

Figure 7.39: Strong head line

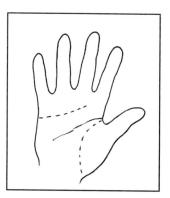

Figure 7.40: Weak head line

122

Figure 7.41: Islanded head line

Figure 7.42: Wavy head line

Figure 7.43: Head line moving straight across hand

Figure 7.44: Head line sloping towards Luna mount

The Simian Line

The single transverse palmar crease or Simian line exists when the heart and head lines join together as one. It appears as a straight line across the palm (Figure 7.46).

The Simian line tends to intensify both the mind and the personality. People with simian lines often alternate between one emotional

Figure 7.45: Head line dropping strongly towards Luna

Figure 7.46: Simian line

extreme and the other, with the feelings often in conflict with the intellect. They have great tenacity of purpose, love hard work, and have a strong capacity for accomplishment.

If the skin texture, mounts, and fingers indicate a coarse personality, the owner of the Simian line can be violent and unpredictable. Be sure to examine the entire hand carefully before making your evaluation.

The Saturn Line

The vertical distal crease or line of Saturn is also known popularly as the fate line, destiny line, career line, or line of life task (Figure 7.1f). This line normally moves upwards from just above the wrist towards the mount of Saturn. More properly called the "line of achievement," it shows the degree to which we have fulfilled our deepest goals in life. It indicates our level of personal success and self-fulfillment as well as recording the obstacles, changes, and restrictions that challenge us during our lifetime.

The implications of this line are highly subjective. A bank president who is frustrated with his career direction can have a weak or broken Saturn line, while the man who cleans his office and is satisfied with his work can have a line that is strong, long, and clear.

Ideally, the Saturn line should be deep, clear, and free of islands, downward branches, or dots. The further up on the hand it begins, the later in life the person finds his or her life's work. Consult Chapter 12 for more about this line.

The Apollo Line

When it appears, this vertical line is found on the mount of Apollo (Figure 7.1g). Long Apollo lines are rare. Most of them consist of a small dash (or a series of overlapping dashes) beginning at the top of the heart line and reaching to slightly below the ring finger. Called the "line of capability" by the famous American palmist William G. Benham, the presence of this line indicates the potential of great achievement in life. It points to honors, success, money, and/or creative ability, especially in areas involving art and music. It can also be a sign of deep personal fulfillment. Many well-known artists, musicians, actors, and writers have a strong line of Apollo, although this line is also found on the hands of people who simply love music, art, and things of beauty.

It is also found on people who are "lucky" in their professional life. They are often the first to be hired for a new job, or have a knack for being at the right place at the right time.

The Mercury Line

Known also as the health or stomach line, the line of Mercury (Figure 7.1h) indicates the degree of balance in the physical organism and its basic nervous state. Ideally, this line should not appear at all, but when it does, it moves from the base of the life line towards the Mercury or little finger. Most people have this line on their palms.

- When deep and free from breaks (Figure 7.47) this line indicates a strong physical constitution and good digestion.
- Breaks in the line (Figure 7.48) reveal stomach and intestinal problems due to nervousness, repressed emotions, or strictly physical factors like poor diet or intestinal parasites. In women, it may also indicate gynecological problems.

 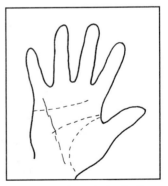

Figure 7.47: Deep line of Mercury, free from breaks

Figure 7.48: Breaks in the line of Mercury

The Line of Neptune

The line of Neptune, or *via lascivia*, is considered one of many "minor lines" of the hand (Figure 7.49a). Its existence has become increasingly common in recent years, and recognizing its presence can be of vital importance to those who have it. This line (also known as "the line of poisons") normally branches off the life line and moves towards the lower mount of Mars or the mount of Luna. It is often weak and broken.

The existence of this line reveals a strong sensitivity to drugs, tobacco, alcohol, and other toxic substances. It is also found on people who are dependent on one or more of these substances, which can also include caffeine and sugar. People who have food allergies often have this line as well.

Many people who have this line need to be very careful when taking either prescribed or over-the-counter medications.

They often have a strong interest in natural therapies like homeopathy and herbal medicine.

Travel Lines

Travel lines (Figure 7.49b) are small horizontal lines located on the outer edge of the palm that move up—according to the time of the trip in relation to the person's age—along the mounts of Luna and Mars towards the heart line.

Each travel line represents an important journey. The

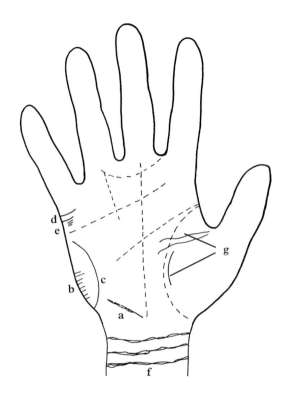

Figure 7.49: Minor lines of the hand

a-Via Lascivia   d-Lines of Union   g-Lines of
b-Travel Lines   e-Children's Lines   Influence
c-Line of Uranus   f-Rascettes

trip may be important in terms of distance, duration, or its overall impact on the life. For a diplomat who is constantly traveling all over the world, a month-long visit to the Far East would probably be of minor importance, while a two-hundred mile journey for a farmer who rarely travels would appear on the hand as a major travel experience. The more important the journey, the longer and deeper the line.

Some people have a line that closely resembles a travel line, but is deeper and longer and located only on the mount of Luna. Although hand readers do not generally agree on its significance, this line appears to be found on people who are extremely fond of adventure and risk, whether physical, psychological, or both.

The Line of Uranus

The line of Uranus (Figure 7.49c) or the *intuitive crescent* begins on the mount of Luna and moves in a gentle arc towards the mount of Mercury, sometimes moving parallel to the Mercury or stomach line.

While this line rarely appears in its perfect form, it indicates powerful intuition with strong psychic abilities. It is often found on the hands of clairvoyants, mediums, and healers. More common in its incomplete state, it appears as a short line moving diagonally across Luna towards the center of the palm.

Lines of Union

These small horizontal lines are found on the mount of Mercury and run from the percussion of the hand towards the inside of the palm (Figure 7.49d). Formerly called "marriage lines," the lines of union indicate important relationships that impress the person deeply. These relationships do not necessarily involve marriage. They can be with either a man or a woman, and may or may not include sex. The stronger the line, the deeper the potential union.

To determine age, measure upwards from the heart line. For example, midway between the heart line and the base of the Mercury finger should be approximately 35 years of age. However, rely on your intuition to determine the exact age.

Children's Lines

The existence and location of so-called children's lines (Figure 7.49e) are subject to controversy. From my experience, they appear as tiny horizontal lines located beneath the lines of union. Like other aspects of the hand, they reveal the *potential* of children only. Miscarriages and abortions would be recorded as potential children.

In general, children's lines can be read with greater accuracy on the hands of women (after all, it is they who give birth to the children), although these lines can also occasionally exist on the hands of men.

Rascettes of Venus

The rascettes (Figure 7.49f) are lines that appear on the underside of the wrist. Each strong, unbroken line is said to represent thirty years of good health. Weak, broken, or chained rascettes reveal a weak physical condition, and in women have been linked to gynecological problems. Be sure to examine other aspects of the hand for confirmation.

Lines of Influence

Lines that run parallel to the vertical lines of the hand—such as those of life, Saturn, and Apollo—strengthen these lines. In many cases, they repair a split or strengthen a section of a line that is islanded or chained (Figure 7.49g).

Lines of influence that emanate from the mount of Venus and move horizontally across the hand generally indicate obstacles, traumas, and times of testing. They are not necessarily negative, because they often record events that provide wisdom and valuable life experience.

If, at the point of crossing a line (usually the life and/or head line) a red dot is formed, a major illness or accident is possible. This would also hold true if an island or break follows the point of crossing. Examine other lines for confirming or modifying indicators.

SKIN RIDGE
PATTERNS

As part of our genetic heritage, every human being possesses a unique pattern of *dermatoglyphics*, the skin ridges of the hands and feet. Taken from the Greek *derma*, meaning "skin," and *glyphe*, meaning "carve," the skin ridge patterns of the fingers and palms are believed to be primarily an anti-slip device and may improve our sense of touch. However, they also can provide important physical and psychological information.

What Skin Patterns Reveal

Because skin ridge patterns are genetically unique, they show basic inherited characteristics, attitudes, and tendencies.

Deciphering these patterns can be an important part of an overall hand analysis.

Not everyone possesses loops, whorls, and other skin ridge patterns on their palms. Palmar ridge patterns are merely an additional guidepost that helps us to achieve a clearer, more specialized understanding of certain human personality traits.

The Raja Loop

The *Raja loop* (also known as the loop of charisma) is found between the Jupiter and Saturn fingers (Figure 8.1). Although extremely rare, it is a good pattern to have, since it reveals a strong ability to lead and inspire others. People with Raja loops often gather a following of devoted admirers or devotees. In addition to successful politicians, entertainers, and religious leaders, people who are considered authorities in

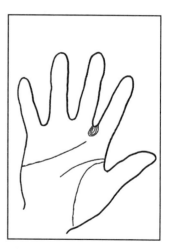

Figure 8.1: The Raja Loop

their chosen field of work or study may have the Raja loop.

The Loop of Seriousness

The *loop of seriousness* (Figure 8.2) is located between the fingers of Saturn and Apollo. It is far more common than the Raja loop, and can be found on approximately twenty percent of all hands. Its presence reveals a serious, responsible, and often ambitious individual. People with this loop tend to have a definite purpose or mission in life. They don't like to waste time, and are sometimes driven towards achieving their career goals.

Figure 8.2. The Loop of Seriousness

Some loops of seriousness can be seen easily with the naked eye, while others require the use of a magnifying glass. Like other skin ridge patterns, the loop of seriousness should be large and well-defined in order to reveal its full meaning.

The Loop of Humor

The *loop of humor* (Figure 8.3) is located between the Apollo and Mercury fingers. Its owners tend to value comfort and pleasure over status and financial rewards. They tend to take life easy; they laugh things off, and have a sense of the ridiculous.

They are apt to choose a profession that provides them with interest and enjoyment over one that pays well. Some of the funniest people I have ever met have loops of humor on their palms.

Figure 8.3: The Loop of Humor

The presence of a loop of seriousness and a loop of humor on the same hand indicates that the individual can have a serious approach to life and the ability to enjoy it at the same time.

The Vanity Loop

The *vanity loop* is somewhat rare. It consists of a large loop that entirely encompasses the Apollo mount (Figure 8.4).

In general, the presence of this loop has one of two meanings:

- Excessive preoccupation with his or her appearance.
- A tendency to be overly sensitive to criticism.

Figure 8.4: The Vanity Loop

The Memory Loop

The so-called *memory loop* is found on perhaps ten per cent of all hands and is located on the radial side of the palm (Figure 8.5). In addition to revealing a good memory (whether for facts or emotional impressions), the presence of this loop is said to provide insight into the minds and motives of others.

When located near the mount of Mars, it reveals a more practical type of

Figure 8.5: The Memory Loop

memory, while deep in the Luna mount, it can indicate psychic ability. It is often found among clairvoyants, astrologers, palmists, and card readers.

The Nature Loop

The *nature loop* (Figure 8.6) is normally located on the percussion of the hand below the start of the heart line. It is often found on people who have a strong love of nature and are inspired by being in a natural environment. They often have a special ability to communicate with animals or plants. This loop can also be found lower in the hand, in the area of the mount of Luna.

Figure 8.6: The Nature Loop

The Empathy Loop

Somewhat uncommon, the *empathy loop* rises from the wrist area just where skin ridge patterns begin on the hand (Figure 8.7). People with this loop take a special interest in others and are able to feel compassion for them.

The Music Loop

The *music loop* can be found towards the bottom of the mount of Venus (Figure 8.8). Although rare, it can occasionally be found along with the "angles" described in Chapter 5. This loop is found on the hands of people who are deeply moved by music. If the loop is clearly marked on both hands, the individual may choose to make music a career, whether as a composer, a musician, or a music teacher.

Figure 8.7: The Empathy Loop

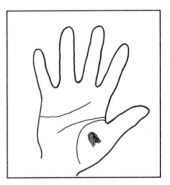

Figure 8.8: The Music Loop

The Bee

The *bee* (Figure 8.9) is found on the hands of people who have a strong love for music made by stringed instruments such as the guitar, cello, or violin. Located near the center of the Venus mount, it is sometimes found on professional musicians who have a special talent for playing stringed instruments.

Figure 8.9: The Bee

The Loop of Courage

The so-called *loop of courage* (Figure 8.10) is rare. When it exists, it is a sign of courage and fearlessness.

Whorl on Luna

A whorl pattern on the mount of Luna (Figure 8.11) is also rare. When it exists, it is a sign of a powerful imagination and a strong ability to visualize.

Figure 8.10: The Loop of Courage

Some palmists feel that it is a sign of clairvoyance and psychic ability.

A Composite Pattern on Luna

A small number of individuals possess a twinned-loop pattern on the mount of Luna, which is sometimes called the "S-bend" pattern (Figure 8.12). Some palmists feel that this pattern is found on people who exhibit psychological traits that are popularly identified with the opposite sex. For example, men with this pattern would tend to be very gentle and sensitive, while women with this pattern would be tough, competitive, and assertive.

Figure 8.11: Whorl on Luna

Figure 8.12: Composite pattern on Luna

Generally speaking, any kind of dermatoglyphic pattern on the Luna mount heightens the person's imaginative, instinctual, and receptive nature.

II

PALMISTRY IN EVERYDAY LIFE

9

BRAINS AND
PERSONALITY

Palmistry can tell us a lot about intelligence, memory, and creative imagination. Unlike modern aptitude tests, which measure only present ability (determined in part by social factors, education, and "test experience"), the hand can reveal both present ability (by locating our age on the head line) and innate potential (by studying the head line and other aspects of the hand together).

Intelligence works on both concrete and abstract levels, and involves a variety of factors.

- understanding what others are saying

- being able to express our ideas to others

- the ability to see similarities and differences between objects and issues

- the ability to work with numbers and compute data

- the capacity to find an underlying rule or structure in a series of events, objects, or numbers
- the ability to remember

The head line is our primary indicator of intelligence, though other factors can reveal the direction and the intensity with which we express intelligence.

The Intelligent Head Line

Basically, the head line shows both the level of our intelligence and how we use it in daily life. This line should be clear, deep, and free of islands, breaks, and dots from beginning to end.

The longer the head line, the greater the intellectual potential and range of intellectual interests. It indicates thinking that is careful, detailed, and comprehensive. An average head line extends to a point under the Apollo finger, while longer lines normally extend to a point under the Mercury finger. Albert Einstein's head line, for example, ran clear across his palm. Another long head line (Figure 9.1), belongs to a woman who scored second in a series of intelligence tests given to 2,800 pre-university students by the New York City Department of Education, placing her in the 99.9 percentile.

Her hand also features a very clear memory loop, located

just under the final quarter of her head line, indicating a superior memory. Another feature that reveals above-average intelligence is a predominance of high loops on the fingertips (see Chapter 6).

Figure 9.1: Handprint showing long, clear head line

Before we gloat or despair (as the case may be) over the length of our head line, remember that a short head line does not necessarily mean a shortage of intelligence, but only thinking that is simple, practical, and to the point. Thought processes tend to be limited to mundane affairs.

The head line can grow longer or shorter over time. My uncle, who is a professor of mathematics, has always had a strong yet relatively short head line. When he started to learn about computers, his head line grew one-half inch within two years. Do we spend our leisure time passively watching game shows or soaps, or do we devote our free time to actively learning about science, history, or philosophy by reading books and studying? The extent to which we use our inherent talents and abilities depends on us!

The clarity and strength of the head line are reliable indicators of present capability.

- A clear, well-defined head line reveals an ability to evaluate concepts and situations, a strong memory, and a clarity of purpose that can lead to concrete action.

- Head lines that are weak, chained, islanded, or fretted (Figure 9.2), reveal a less "grounded" type of mental energy, which undermines clear thinking and diminishes our capacity to focus and act.

Figure 9.2: Handprint showing weak, fretted head line

Islands

Islands on the head line have several meanings. They indicate confusion, difficulty in concentration, and the tendency to be scatterbrained. Neurotic behavior, such as anxiety, phobias, or depression may be indicated, although this can be found in people with every type of head line. Islands on the head line may also be related to the abuse of drugs or alcohol, being the cause, the result, or both. As a rule, the larger the island, the more serious the mental or emotional difficulty.

When the island begins where an influence line from the Mars or Venus mount cuts the head line (Figure 9.3), chances are that a powerful trauma or other event set off a period of psychological difficulty. By the same token, an influence line may appear at the end of an island, indicating that the event or its effect brought the period of difficulty to an end. When the influence line leaves a dot on the head line, the cause of mental or psychological weakness is primarily physical in origin—the result of an accident or illness affecting the body directly.

Figure 9.3: Island on head line formed by influence line

Breaks

Breaks on the head line indicate periods of transition. A quick break (Figure 9.5) would be immediate, possibly the result of an accident or some other trauma. When lines overlap for a time (Figure 9.4), the changes are more gradual.

The quality of the head line at the point of the break provides a good indication of how the person reacts to the transition. Often when we experience a period of difficulty, we view it only in a negative way, while in reality it may open the door to important insights and new opportunities. When going through a difficult emotional transition, we need to recognize the positive aspects of our dilemma and be encouraged to overcome the obstacles and move forward. Since the lines in the hand change—breaks in the head line especially—such encouragement can be a real service to the person seeking our help as hand consultants.

Figure 9.4: Overlaps on the head line

Figure 9.5: Breaks on the head line

The Creative Mind

Creativity is closely related to intelligence, although it reflects the personality more than intellect does. Creativity is primarily a measure of *divergent thinking* (How many uses can you find for a kitchen knife?) rather than *convergent thinking* (What is the capital of Australia?).

Certain skin ridge patterns have been linked with creativity. A predominance of whorls on the fingertips is a sign of an original, independent, and unconventional thinker. A whorl on the Apollo finger alone is a sign of artistic ability, and is found on the hands of many graphic artists, architects, designers, and painters. As mentioned before, any unusual skin ridge pattern on the mount of Luna (the seat of the imagination) reveals a strong instinctual nature and a fertile, imaginative mind. The handprint in Figure 9.6 is a good example. It belongs to a highly talented American jeweler/designer. His entire Luna mount is covered with thick, swirling skin ridges.

The Creative Head Line

Like intelligence, the primary measure of creativity is the head line. However, it is the form of the line—rather than its length—that determines how intellectual ability is applied, and whether the person's creativity is grounded or scattered.

Figure 9.6: Handprint revealing a strong creative nature and imaginative mind

- A *wavy* head line (Figure 9.7) reveals an original (and often unusual) mind that can conceive new ideas and unconventional points of view.

- A *straight* head line (Figure 9.8) may either run across the hand or slope downwards. It indicates clear and concentrated thinking regardless of the direction in which it moves.

- A *curved* head line (Figure 9.9) reveals a mind that likes to experiment and play with new ideas.

Generally speaking, a head line that moves straight across the palm indicates a strong convergent mind. While its owners may possess abundant information, they have a

Figure 9.7: A wavy head line

Figure 9.8: A straight head line

tendency to view the world primarily in practical terms. Imagination and creativity play a relatively minor role. People with this type of line like to follow rules and dislike innovation. Their realistic, practical traits are often strengthened if their hands are rigid and the fingers are squarish in form.

Figure 9.9: A curved head line

A creative head line should slope gently downwards towards the mount of Luna, which indicates a balance between realistic and imaginative thought processes.

When the line ends in a small fork, this sense of balance is strengthened, and there is a union of practical and imaginative ideas with an ability to see both sides of an issue. When this branch is extremely long and wide (Figure 9.10), it indicates more a split between these two worlds.

Figure 9.10: Large branch at end of head line

The more the head line slopes towards the mount of Luna, the greater the divergent or imaginative thought processes. To learn whether or not the imagination is well-grounded, we must ask the questions below.

When the head line literally plunges towards Luna (Figure 9.11), you can be sure that the imagination is extremely strong. Like other aspects of the hand, this sign

Figure 9.11: Head line plunging towards Luna mount

IMAGINATION CHECKLIST

- Is the head line strong or broken or chained?
- Does the flexibility of the hand show emotional stability?
- Does the space between the life and head lines show thinking before acting?
- Are the fingers conic, square, or spatulate?
- Is the Saturn line strong or weak?

---

has both positive and negative connotations. People with drooping head lines are able to come up with creative ideas and solutions to problems that others cannot. Yet, when facing a problem, their imagination can blow it way out of proportion.

Islands or breaks in this type of head line indicate that the person could go off the deep end into a world of fantasy. If the space between the head and heart lines is narrow, the fantasy world is more secret and internalized. When coupled with a bent Saturn finger (indicating depressive tendencies), strong feelings of depression and fantasy can lead to suicidal thoughts. If a drooping head line contains islands or breaks towards the end, psychotic behavior can become evident later in life.

If a drooping head line is broken or fragmented (Figure 9.12), the person may become suicidal. If you are reading the hand of someone with this type of head line, tactfully verify your suspicion by asking questions. Refer the individual to a competent professional, if possible.

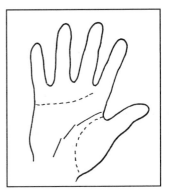

Figure 9.12: Fragmented head line

Signs of Mental Illness

Can we diagnose mental illness from the hand? Several books, particularly *The Hands of Children* by Julius Speer and *The Hand in Psychological Diagnosis* by Dr. Charlotte Wolff, are devoted to the study of mental patients. Although written decades ago, they are still valuable sources of reference.

It is difficult to make a specific psychological diagnosis from the hand. In the first place, it is well documented that normally rational and well-balanced people are capable of irrational, bizarre, and even violent behavior when undergoing extreme duress.

In addition, society has long placed a label of "crazy" or "deviant" on individuals who do not conform to its established standards. Some of the most creative individuals in history—including numerous composers, inventors, writers, and artists—were condemned as mad by their contemporaries, only later to be recognized as creative geniuses.

It is also important to avoid generalizations based on actions alone. For example, is a man who cuts his wrists in a suicide attempt very different from another who commits suicide by eating the wrong foods even though his doctor advises him to abstain? Their hands may reveal different currents (the former's hand may include a classic "suicidal head line," while the latter's hand may appear completely normal).

We need to consider the hand as a *total unit* rather than make judgments based on one or two aspects alone. Whether

CHECKLIST FOR POSSIBLE MENTAL ILLNESS

- Hands and fingers that are abnormally small or large when compared to the individual's body size.

- Jupiter and Saturn fingers that are of equal length, or Saturn and Apollo fingers that are of equal length. Dr. Wolff found that such configurations appear primarily among schizophrenic patients.

- Any finger that is abnormally short in comparison to the rest (such as a Jupiter finger that does not reach the top phalange of Saturn).

- Fingers that are severely twisted or deformed (especially the Mercury finger) when not the result of arthritis or accident.

- Severely chained, broken, or islanded head lines.

- Head lines that are missing (especially in both hands) or lines that are extremely weak.

- Hands, fingers, and/or fingertips that are extremely rigid or hyper-flexible.

- A thumb that is abnormally short, deformed, or placed extremely high on the hand so that it looks like that of an infant.

- A Simian line found on a poorly shaped hand, or on a hand featuring one or more of the characteristics listed above.

we choose to read hands as a hobby or professionally, we need to strive to be as respectful, open-minded, and non-judgmental as possible.

The hands reveal *potential*. We each determine how we will express this potential in life. A woman with a very long Jupiter finger, for example, can be dictatorial and overbearing. Another woman with a similar characteristic can develop the positive aspects of Jupiter and become a revered spiritual leader.

However, there are several major indicators on the hand that can show the potential for mental illness.

Note: The presence of one or two of the traits in the checklist on page 157 does not mean that the individual is mentally ill. As mentioned before, the features of the hand reveal *potential,* which is always subject to change. In addition, modifying factors in the hand have been known to counteract negative qualities found in its shape, fingers, and lines.

Whenever we find signs of difficulty in the hand, remember that apparent difficulties often open the door to opportunities that lead to experience, transformation, and self-realization.

Will: From Inertia to Action

Will is a divine aspect of the universe and a potent source of strength and power. It enables a plant to break through concrete as it grows, and gives many animal species their tenacious and often uncanny ability to adapt and flourish in a hostile environment.

In humans, will stands behind our ability to survive, to grow, and to manifest our talents and abilities. Without will, humanity would not have been able to evolve. It is the power that helps us explore new horizons and create cities, nations, and civilizations.

Will is concerned with our awareness of ourselves as distinct human beings capable of love, creativity, and self-realization. In esoteric philosophy, it is taught that we possess two egos: the *mortal* or *personal* ego, which governs the basic needs and desires of the personality, and the *divine* ego, which represents the spirit, the "Christ within," or the higher self.

On the most elementary level, will is closely connected with the mortal ego, and represents our basic instinct to survive. In addition to the will to live, we also exert will in order to achieve and maintain the family structure.

As expressed through the mortal ego, will is also involved in more complex psychological issues, including our need for pleasure, power, status, and security. Will is often connected with issues of control, possessiveness, and domination in the family structure, especially with one's spouse and children. When expressed in the context of the workplace, will can manifest as greed, competition, or leadership. In a social environment, will can involve the struggle to obtain social benefits, such as status, popularity, and respect.

As we become more mature on a personality level—and when soul energies transmute from lower levels to higher levels of consciousness—the energy of will changes to reflect more of the divine ego. This level is more connected with feelings of inclusiveness, the application of inner wisdom, and the ability to be open to God's will. The more harmoniously the personal ego can work with the higher self, the greater the degree of personal integration, inner peace, and self-fulfillment.

Will in the Hand

We can see the expression of will in the hand. It is primarily reflected by the strength, form, and position of the thumb, the power of the mounts, and the clarity and scope of the major lines. By understanding our strengths and weaknesses—and by transforming any negative currents into positive core qualities—we can harness the power of will and make it work for us.

Hands of the elementary, square, and spatulate types often reflect a strong will, especially if they are firm, strong, and moderately pliable. Narrow, pale, or overly-soft hands with weak or flexible fingers generally indicate emotional instability, lack of resolve, and difficulty in standing up to adversity.

The Thumb: Ego Incarnate

The thumb represents our individuality and the ability to assert ourselves in the world. On a purely physical level, the opposed thumb sets us apart from other animals—including the apes—and gives us the ability to perform such tasks as construction, mechanics, and surgery, which no other species can accomplish. Without this type of thumb, our ability to communicate, repair, build, invent, and create would be greatly diminished.

On a psychological level, the thumb represents the power of the ego, both on "mortal" and "divine" levels. It symbolizes the strength of our individuality, and our capacity to express our desires, aspirations, and talents in daily life.

We know that infants tend to hide their thumbs from the world until they reach a point in their development when they feel more comfortable in their environment. Adults, going through periods of fear or extreme stress, often cover their thumbs with the other fingers in a regression to their protected lives as infants.

The more prominent the thumb, the greater the ego strength. A long, firm and "expressive" thumb reveals courage, stability, and willpower. The fingertips add character and direction to the thumb. A spatulate tip, for example, reveals an individual of action, who likes to throw himself into business deals, creative projects, and all kinds of adventures. A squarish tip shows that the ego will probably express itself in organizational and administrative affairs, while a conic fingertip would favor artistic ability and the desire to create, whether it be a sculpture, a musical composition, or a computer program.

Skin Ridge Patterns on the Thumb

Skin ridge patterns on the thumb can reveal aspects of will.

- An arch pattern on the thumb reveals a practical, commonsense approach where action is concerned. People with arches on their thumbprints are "doers."

- A whorl print on the thumb tends to strengthen willpower. It is often found on people who are apt to be abrupt and independent in their way of doing things.

- A loop fingerprint on the thumb has no special significance in regard to will. It represents middle-of-the-road qualities of adaptability, emotional responsiveness, and mental elasticity.

- On the surface, a composite loop would be seen to decrease will power, because it reveals a person who may have trouble making decisions. However, it can also be a sign of strength, because such individuals take the time to evaluate a problem in great detail.

After they have made their decision based on the information they've collected, they can be extremely stubborn and tenacious in reaching their goal.

Other Thumb Features

A short, thin, flat, and "waisted" thumb generally reveals a lack of self-confidence and self-assertion. Such individuals tend to underestimate their talents and abilities and have difficulty overcoming adversity.

While a flexible thumb reveals adaptability, generosity, and spontaneity, it can also be a sign of poor will power. People with flexible thumbs often have a difficult time sticking to a diet or adhering to a budget. However, a weak thumb can be strengthened by a hand of firm consistency, limited flexibility, strong mounts of Mars and Venus, and a long, prominent Jupiter finger.

In general, the longer the phalange of will, the greater the will power and the ability to put thoughts into practice. The phalanges of the thumb are discussed in greater detail in Chapter 4.

The position of the thumb is also important. The further the thumb is held from the other four fingers, the greater the degree of courage, self-confidence, and independence. Strong thumbs that separate from the hand at an angle of sixty degrees or more, are found on many executives, military leaders, and others who need to make decisions and stand behind them.

Conversely, a high-set thumb located close to the rest of the hand reveals more contracted personalities who find it difficult to stand up and assert themselves, especially if the thumb is also short, thin, or flat.

The Modifiers

While the thumb is the principal indicator of ego strength and will power, other aspects of the hand can reveal important information which can modify the essential qualities that the thumb reveals.

A Jupiter finger that is longer than the Apollo can strengthen the thumb. Egotism, optimism, and the ability to lead and inspire (as functions of will) are several of the qualities indicated by a strong Jupiter finger.

The desire to stand apart from others and prove oneself can often be revealed by a wider space between Jupiter and Saturn than is found between the other fingers of the hand.

When the head and life lines are separate at their commencement, the power of Jupiter is increased. The individual has a greater ability to inspire, execute, and act in a natural leadership role. There is also a greater degree of self-confidence and self-reliance.

When the lines are connected, a long Jupiter finger

LEADERSHIP AND CONFIDENCE CHECKLIST

- A strong Jupiter mount—one that is more elevated than the other upper mounts of the hand—increases self-confidence and leadership ability. A Raja loop or loop of charisma would enhance these personal qualities.

- A strong Saturn mount enhances emotional stability and thoroughness. Ambition, seriousness, and the will to succeed in life can also be revealed by a clearly marked loop of seriousness located between the Saturn and Apollo fingers.

- A prominent mount of upper Mars increases courage and resistance, especially when the individual is confronted by outside pressures. When this mount is weak or soft, the person has difficulty standing up for himself and can be easily controlled by others.

- A strong mount of lower Mars (it often appears as a raised pad or "tumor" on the palm) is a sign of assertiveness. If in the form of a callous (especially if reddish in color), it reveals aggression and a strong temper.

- A prominent mount of Venus imparts more energy and power to the thumb, strengthening the ability to move forward and create.

would indicate a need for domination and control. The strong ego is eroded by lack of confidence, which is an expression of weak will. The message is "I have to be the boss, or someone else will dominate me." The person needs to be on top of a situation rather than open to the natural flow and movement of life.

The mounts and related skin ridge patterns can also strengthen and detract from the qualities of a strong thumb.

When evaluating a hand, it is important to offer an integrated view. We need to focus on the truth of what we see and, when appropriate, offer guidance to help the person whose hand we are reading resolve areas of weakness or difficulty. In addition, we need to bear in mind that negative traits as revealed in the hand are often distortions of positive core qualities.

For example, a long Jupiter finger can reveal a dominating and controlling personality. However, with awareness and resolve, these traits can be transformed into an ability to inspire and lead others to discover their own inner strengths and abilities. A stiff thumb may indicate stubbornness and inflexibility, but it can also reflect an inner stability that may be open to change. A high-set thumb may indicate fear and a reluctance to experience life, yet it can also reflect a healthy caution and a quiet sense of self-worth.

10

HEALTH IN
YOUR HAND

According to the World Health Organization of the
United Nations (WHO), health is "a state of full physical, psychological, and social well-being, not just the
absence of disease or incapacity."

Dorland's Medical Dictionary agrees, and adds that health
is a state or condition of wholeness, in which all body parts
and functions are coordinating properly.

Our level of health is determined partly by heredity, but
mostly on how we are able to adapt to our environment:
fighting germs, dealing with stress, avoiding accidents,
and resisting environmental pollution. A healthy diet,
stress management, a positive mental attitude, adequate

rest, and regular exercise are seen as major factors in achieving and maintaining good health.

The hand is like a complex puzzle that can change constantly. By understanding individual characteristics—like temperature, consistency, or lines—and making both mental and intuitive connections regarding their relationship with each other, you can use the hand as an ongoing guide to insure your good health and the well-being of those who seek your aid as a hand analyst. By periodically taking handprints and completing a Hand Analysis Test Chart (see page 489), you can keep detailed records of the hand over a period of years. This will enable you to observe changes as they relate to health.

Texture, Temperature, and Color

Doctors have always considered skin texture and temperature a reliable barometer of mood, disposition, age, and health. When people are healthy, happy, and young, their skin is smooth, elastic, and warm. And when they are old, sick, or have a bad disposition, their skin texture is often wrinkled and coarse, or cold and clammy.

Texture

Skin texture is determined by our hormones, which also

control our personality. This is why skin texture is such a useful indicator of our inner nature.

- If the skin is soft and fine, it reflects both physical and psychological vulnerability vis-à-vis the environment. The person is impressionable and refined.

- A coarser skin texture would indicate an individual whose health is not strongly influenced by external factors like temperature, food, noise, and air pollution.

- Dry, rough, scaly hands indicate an underactive thyroid gland, while overly smooth and satiny hands can be a sign of an overactive thyroid. Soft, pudgy fingers, which take on the appearance of sausages, may indicate thyroid problems as well.

Temperature

The temperature of the skin provides information about changes in the blood circulation. In winter, if people's hands remain cold despite warm indoor temperatures, or if the hand is consistently cold in any temperature, there may be a constriction of the tiny blood vessels of the hand. If peoples' hands are cold and clammy, they may be nervous (especially if their hands are being read for the first time). Find out whether the anxiety is temporary or chronic, because clammy hands can also be an indication of insomnia. If the hands (especially the fingers) are cold—even on a warm day—poor circulation may be present, especially if the nails take on a bluish tinge.

Color

The normal color of the palm is rosy and pinkish (regardless of race or skin pigmentation), which testifies to good blood circulation and normal body functioning.

- *Extreme redness* indicates excessive blood circulation in the hands and can point to a predisposition towards high blood pressure, diabetes, gout, heart disease, or stroke.

- *Pallid skin* usually indicates a state of anxiety or anemia. In severe cases, it may be due to internal bleeding. If you bend the hand back and the main crease lines are pale, an iron deficiency may be present.

- *Warm, bluish hands* reveal poor blood circulation or possible heart disease, including congestive heart failure and congenital heart disease. They have also been linked to Reynaud's disease (a condition caused by an abnormal degree of spasm of the blood vessels of the hands and feet), atherosclerosis, and certain adverse drug reactions.

- *Cold, bluish hands* are a sign that the circulatory problem is more localized. Consult a health professional for proper diagnosis and treatment.

- *Yellowish hands* are relatively uncommon, but are a probable indicator of liver disease, including hepatitis and jaundice. However, before you reach such dire conclusions, find out about the person's diet. Yellowish hands are often found among those who consume large amounts of carrot juice!

Hand Consistency and Health

The consistency of the hand is a valuable indicator of health, because it helps us determine our amount of energy.

- *Flabby, soft hands* lack muscle tone and are often small, broad, and bland to the touch. People with flabby or very soft hands tend to over-indulge in life's pleasures, including food, alcohol, and sex. This tendency is especially pronounced if the hands are thick. Owners of such hands are often lazy and have difficulty sustaining will power, particularly if the thumb is flexible or weak.

- *Thin, flat,* and *weak hands* reveal a lack of energy and difficulty sustaining long-term activity. People with these hands are very susceptible to disease and are more prone to vitamin deficiencies than others.

- *Firm hands* are more muscular. They reveal an energetic, strong, and active person who leads a more balanced life. While showing a high degree of responsibility and self-restraint, firm hands also characterize a person who can adapt to unexpected circumstances and be open to new and unfamiliar ideas. As a result, people with firm hands are more resistant to disease than others.

- *Hard* or *rigid hands* do not bend under pressure. Unlike the firm hand, which indicates balance and adaptability, the rigid hand portrays an inflexible, contracted individual with lots of pent-up energy. People with rigid hands need to move their energy out in constructive ways—through sports, gardening, or other activities—in order to avoid stress-related problems like hypertension, stroke, heart disease, ulcers, migraines, and back pain.

The Lines

The lines in the hand are formed at the same time as the skin ridge patterns—during the third and fourth months of the child's life as a fetus. Yet, as we have already seen, while skin ridge patterns stay the same, the lines in the hand can change over time. The lines indicate several important aspects of physical, emotional, and mental health:

- our degree of emotional balance and expression
- our level of physical vitality

- our vulnerability to trauma, including illness, accidents, and close calls with death.

The Life Line

Of all the lines in the hand, the life line or the line of vitality is the one that most people are concerned about. The life line is the first to develop in embryonic life, and its depth, clarity, and length reveal our level of vitality and physical constitution.

As pointed out earlier, the line of life begins approximately where the thumb meets the index finger and moves downwards towards the wrist. The top of the line begins at the time of birth, while the bottom (where it begins to curve around the base of the thumb ball near the wrist) is at approximately seventy years of age. As the central line of the hand (everybody has it), the life line records all important events, including major diseases, brushes with death, major life transitions, traumas, and loss of strength and vitality.

The broken life line in Figure 10.1 indicates a life-threatening operation when the individual was in her mid-twenties. The young woman barely survived the operation. Her close call with death had a profound effect on her attitude towards life, and led to greater creativity and personal freedom.

Since the life line can change, future life events and indications of illness are subject to change. One case in point: the print of a thirty-four year old lawyer (Figure 10.2) shows his

Figure 10.1: Handprint showing broken life line with inner life line

life line was broken at approximately sixty years of age, which could indicate a life-threatening disease. Concerned about this possibility, he decided to improve his diet and cut down on smoking. Within several years, the line mended completely, as seen in Figure 10.3. The possibility of a serious disease helped him to adopt positive lifestyle habits. He took responsibility for his health *before* symptoms appeared.

A long, clear, and deep life line (Figure 10.3) indicates vitality and a strong constitution, while a short or weak life line full of islands and breaks (Figure 10.4) reveals constitutional weakness and vulnerability to disease. People with this type of line often have less power to endure and resist diseases or injuries.

This type of life line does not automatically condemn us to a short life or ill health. But it does indicate that we should not take our health for granted.

Islands on the life line often indicate periods of low vitality and increased vulnerability to disease. If they happen to correspond in time with islands on the head, heart, or career line, they can indicate confusion, worry, or lack of direction and focus. An egg-shaped island at the end of the life line is sometimes found on the hands of people with cancer. While this is not a guarantee that one will suffer from cancer, it may indicate a genetic predisposition to the disease. However, many people with cancer do not have this feature on the life line at all.

Figure 10.2: Handprint showing clear, broken life line

Figure 10.3: Same handprint showing mended life line

Figure 10.4: Handprint showing weak life line

People with this island needn't panic, but simply eliminate the proven contributory factors that can lead to cancer.

Red or blue dots appearing on the life line often indicate a serious illness or an accident involving a high fever. If a corresponding dot appears on the heart, head, or stomach line at the same age, that organ will most likely be affected, especially if the dot appears on both hands.

If the life line is broken by an influence line coming from the mount of Venus, a serious accident may be indicated. Check both hands for verification.

Supporting Lines

The *inner life line* (Figure 10.1), which runs parallel to the life line (see page 174), provides added strength during illness, accident, or loss of vitality. In the print, this short line "covers" the break in the life line, and modifies its effect.

At times the *Saturn* or *fate line* takes over the task of a weak or disappearing life line (Figure 10.5). In this case, the Saturn line does "double duty" as a supplementary life line and an indicator of career direction.

The Head Line

A good *head line* is clear, strong, and free from islands and breaks. From a health perspective, islands indicate periods of

Figure 10.5: Handprint showing Saturn line

worry or indecision that can lead to tension and stress-related diseases. If you have an island or break in your head line, you need to avoid mental stress or aggravation during the time period indicated on the line. Eat foods that relax rather than stimulate, avoid caffeine and refined sugars, and give yourself frequent periods of relaxation, recreation, and meditation.

The Heart Line

A person who is physically or mentally ill is usually emotionally disturbed. Therefore, to evaluate health, we also need to examine the line of the heart.

In our age of anxiety, the heart line is the most vital one of all. It is the barometer of the emotions, and reveals how (and to what extent) we give and receive love and affection.

Much can be said about the psychological significance of this important line, but here we shall deal only with the diagnostic value of the heart line in reference to cardiac diseases.

Ideally, the heart line should be deep, clear, and well-formed, with a minimum of islands, breaks, and chains. Very often the heart line tends to be chained near its beginning, which can indicate emotional and possibly sexual turmoil, especially during youth.

In *Medical Palmistry*, Dr. Scheimann advised that whenever we examine a heart line and discover abnormalities, we should avoid diagnosing heart ailments. He felt that only a physician can do that. To find out whether an ill-formed or broken heart line is an indication of a heart ailment, study the nails and the life line.

See if the nails are clubbed and the base of the nails are blue. If either or both of these signs are present, you can suspect heart disease.

In addition, check for unevenness in the life line. Determine whether it splits or breaks or is crossed by a line that runs from the defect on the heart line to the life line. If you fail to find any of these health defects, the mark on the heart line is more likely to reveal emotional problems than physical disease.

Changes in the palmar ridges

Figure 10.6: Nodules on heart line. From Eugene Scheimann, M.D. and Nathaniel Altman, *Medical Palmistry* (Aquarian, 1989).

Dr. Scheimann observed that the nodules that occur in coronary heart disease (Figure 10.6) are often associated with an island on the heart line. If you find any kind of defect (such as a break, a chain, bluish dots, or an island) on the heart line below the little finger or the ring finger, consider it a possible sign of disease, especially if the individual also exhibits certain contributory factors such as anxiety, overweight, high cholesterol, or high blood pressure. Also examine the dermatoglyphic patterns (especially the axial triradius described later on in this chapter). If you find any abnormalities, remind the person of the heart line defect and advise him or her to be conscious of the need for a low-fat high-fiber diet, proper exercise, and stress management.

Blue or reddish dots on the heart line are possible indications of heart trouble or circulatory disease.

The Mercury Line

This line begins near the end of the life line and moves upwards diagonally towards the little (or Mercury) finger, (Figure 10.7). It has also

Figure 10.7: Handprint showing broken line of Mercury

been called the "health line," "stomach line," and "hepatic line." Ideally, it is better not to have this line in the hand at all, since its presence indicates a predisposition to problems of the stomach, intestines, liver, kidneys, and female reproductive organs. The print in Figure 10.7 is from a young man suffering from severe colitis, which eventually required a colostomy. Liver disease is often recognized by a yellowish tinge to the nails or skin in addition to a broken Mercury line.

While a strong, clear Mercury line indicates a greater degree of resistance to such problems, a weak, fragmented line could reveal existing or potential stomach ulcers, intestinal problems (including colitis), chronic constipation, glandular problems, or other disorders.

These problems may be due to genetic, emotional, or purely physical causes, but in my experience I have found them to be primarily of emotional origin. The abdomen and the solar plexus have been called "the mirror of the emotions." When we repress feelings of anger, grief, and frustration, they can implode and cause abdominal pain and dysfunction.

The Via Lascivia

Although not a major line on the hand, the *via lascivia* (or line of Neptune) branches off the life line and moves below and often parallel to the line of Mercury. It is often weak and broken (Figure 10.8). This line is often found on individuals who have a strong sensitivity to drugs (both prescribed and illegal), alcohol, tobacco, and other substances. Food allergies are common, as is a tendency to become addicted to substances like tobacco, sugar, or caffeine. It is a common line on the hands of drug addicts and alcoholics. (See page 128.)

Figure 10.8: Hand print showing the *Via Lascivia*

Skin Ridges and Health

As pointed out earlier, our hands are patterned with various systems of parallel rows of dermatoglyphics that are unique for each human being. Where these ridges meet, they form a *triradius*. Four distinct triradii are found just under (and sometimes between) the fingers above the heart line, which we have already described as an apex of each of the various mounts. In addition, there is one major triradius (known as the *axial triradius*) located at the base of the palm just above the wrist. A triradius in its normal position is reproduced in Figure 10.9. According to the *Journal of the American Medical Association*, when the axial triradius appears at a higher location, it can indicate a predisposition to congenital heart disease.

Figure 10.9: Normal axial triradius

Another sign of possible heart disease exists when previously normal fingers tend towards "clubbing" (Figure 10.10). Although clubbed fingers may be an inherited trait, their presence—especially with watch-glass or Hippocratic nails (discussed on page 192)—indicates a tendency towards heart and lung disorders. When accompanied by a displaced axial triradius, present or potential heart disease is a good possibility.

Abnormal skin ridge patterns have been linked to over seventy different diseases, including irritable

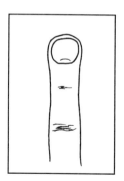

Figure 10.10: Clubbed finger

bowel syndrome, rubella syndrome, thyroid cancer, Alzheimer's disease, sex chromosome disorders, and congenital abnormalities like Down's syndrome. Other medical studies have linked diabetes mellitus, spontaneous abortion, cerebral palsy, epilepsy, leukemia, and schizophrenia with abnormal skin ridge patterns. Whorls or loops on the mount of Luna, an abnormal number of skin ridges on the fingers, the presence of whorls on all ten fingers, composite fingerprint patterns on all ten fingers, and unusual placement of the apexes on the palm may all indicate the presence of congenital abnormalities.

Differentiating normal ridge patterns from abnormal ones involves a great deal of knowledge and expertise. Until you become proficient in hand analysis, it's a good idea to refrain from making a health diagnosis based on the skin ridge patterns.

However, there is one skin ridge feature that is easy to see. It involves *disassociated skin ridge patterns*, known in palmistry as the String of Pearls. It is compared with a normal skin ridge pattern in Figure 10.11. The presence of a disassociated skin ridge patterns is often a sign of present or impending poor health. A string of pearls can be found on people who are dealing poorly with stress, vitamin deficiency, or with a disease like diabetes or cancer. In our studies of the hands of people with AIDS, Dr. Scheimann and I found that every single case had disassociated ridge patterns to some extent.

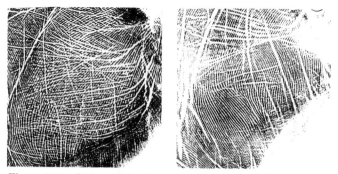

Figure 10.11: String of Pearls compared to normal ridge pattern

We have also found that when health improves, the disassociated ridges can become "associated" once again, even among individuals whose health was threatened by the HIV virus. One person began acupuncture treatments and made positive changes in his diet, attitudes, and lifestyle. As his T-cell count improved, his skin ridges became more associated. Whenever you find a string of pearls on the hand, be sure to check the nails and the life line in order to make a more accurate and complete evaluation.

Disassociated ridge patterns can also reveal mental or emotional problems.

It should be no surprise that the hand reveals both psychological and physical illness. The discovery of neuropeptides—the "communication modules" in the brain and body that regulate our moods and emotions—has led researchers to believe that the mind and body are inseparable.

The Nails in Medical Diagnosis

The nails are the first tissues of the body surface to develop, and sometimes appear as early as the ninth week of prenatal life.

In addition to the nails' revealing certain personality traits, medical doctors have used it as an aid in diagnosing endocrine disturbances, circulatory problems, anemia, and other diseases. Although medical diagnosis through the nails is still a relatively young science, careful examination of the nails can tell you many things about character and health and should be a part of every hand analysis. However, be sure to corroborate your findings with other signs on the hand before making a final evaluation.

Color

The color of the nails can be an important indicator of disease or deficiency.

- *Pink nails* that are smooth and lustrous reveal a balanced mental disposition, adequate nutritional intake, and good general health.

- *Reddish nails* indicate stronger blood circulation, and a tendency towards flashes of anger, over-excitement, and high blood pressure. People with red-dish nails need to avoid caffeine and other stimulants, and learn how to release pent-up emotions through exercise, creative activity, and regular meditation.

- *Blue* or *bluish nails* indicate circulatory problems. If all the nails on both hands are bluish, the disturbance is more a problem of the circulatory system as a whole, while several blue or bluish nails reveal a more local-ized problem in the hands or fingers. If the nails are bluish and the person has no circulatory complaints, chances are that the personality is somewhat reserved and cold. Warmth and passion are hidden behind a facade of cool equilibrium and restraint. Bodywork, the martial arts, and other dynamic exercise tech-niques are often useful in increasing blood circulation to the extremities and help us express our emotions more directly and fully.

- *Pale nails*—like pale skin—indicate low vitality and poor nutrition.

- *Yellowish nails* may reveal liver trouble.

- *Brownish nails* are an indicator of malnutrition and injury to the nervous system.

- *Slate gray nails* can reveal the presence of malaria.

- Nail beds that are *amber* in color can indicate syphilis.

Other indications:

- *White dots* or *spots* on the nails are general signs of anxiety or stress, and are often found on individuals who suffer from chronic depression. They may also indicate a calcium deficiency, especially if the nails are soft.

- *Moons* should ideally appear on all the fingernails and indicate good health and a strong constitution. Their absence altogether may indicate an underactive thyroid gland (especially if the nails are brittle, ridged, and short), while abnormally large moons (moons that fill over a third of the nail surface) indicate general weakness and an overactive thyroid gland.

Shapes

- *Fan-shaped* or *long, narrow nails* (Figures 10.12 and 10.13) reveal an individual prone to chronic nervousness with a low tolerance for frustration. People with these nails usually are prone to suffer from nervous disorders and psychosomatic diseases.

- *Short nails* (Figure 10.14) are often found on individuals who are highly critical. They are impa-

Figure 10.12: Fan-shaped nail

Figure 10.13: Long, narrow nail

Figure 10.14: Short nail

tient towards themselves, other people, and life in general. Heart trouble, high blood pressure, and depression have been linked to short nails on most or all of the fingers.

- *Hippocratic* or *watch-glass nails* (Figure 10.15) are lustrous and curved in the shape of a watch crystal. They indicate a general weakness of the respiratory system, and have been found on people who are heavy smokers or sufferers of tuberculosis or other lung diseases. Hippocratic nails can also reveal a predisposition to heart disease (especially if the nails are bluish in color) and cirrhosis of the liver (especially if the nails are yellowish in color). Whenever you see people with watch-glass nails (even when the curvature is mild), verify if they are smokers. You may want to advise that they stop smoking or seek out as pollution-free an environment as possible.

- *Spoon nails* (Figure 10.16) are concave in appearance and reveal nutritional deficiencies (especially in iron), an underactive thyroid gland, and the possible presence of chronic skin disorders.

Figure 10.15: Watchglass or Hippocratic nail

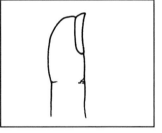

Figure 10.16: Spoon nail

Lines, Ridges, and Other Signs

Healthy nails are well-proportioned in size, strong without being brittle, pink in color, and have between 75 and 100 fine parallel shallow ridges moving vertically from the base of the nail (the nail bed) to the top.

- *Beau's lines* (Figure 10.17) are deep horizontal ridges or "dents" that begin at the base of the nail and move upwards as the nail grows. They are associated with nervous shock, acute infections, nutritional deficiencies, and other physical and emotional traumas.
- *Mee's lines* (Figure 10.18) are similar to Beau's lines, but do not form dents on the nail surface. They are considered to be indicators of high fever, arsenic poisoning, and coronary heart disease.
- *Longitudinal ridges* (Figure 10.19) are often associated with chronic diseases like colitis, long-standing skin disorders, rheumatism, and hyper thyroidism.
- *Soft nails* that split easily often indicate some kind of

Figure 10.17: Beau's lines   **Figure 10.18: Mee's lines**   **Figure 10.19: Longitudinal ridges**

nutritional deficiency (especially in protein and calcium). They are often found on people suffering from arthritis.

- *Brittle and broken nails* can be a sign of an underactive thyroid or pituitary gland.

Although there is no foolproof technique for diagnosing disease, a careful and thorough study of the human hand can provide a wealth of information regarding predispositions to a wide variety of disease conditions and the actual presence of disease or deficiency. Medical palmistry can be of tremendous value—either alone or in conjunction with other diagnostic techniques—to make us aware of what prevents us from enjoying optimum health. Since it is *the body that heals itself*, hand analysis can guide us towards taking personal responsibility for our health and adopting lifestyle habits that will enable us to enjoy more healthy, active, and productive lives.

11

LOVE, RELATIONSHIP, AND SEXUALITY

Palmistry can reveal important information to help us understand both who we are as sexual beings and how we can enjoy satisfying romantic and sexual relationships with others.

Relationship is essential for both spiritual progress and psychological well-being. While we all need—and deserve—time by ourselves, the quality and quantity of our relationships with others are a mirror of our own state of being. They can also be a reliable guide to our degree of personal integration and fulfillment.

How can our hands help us with relationships?

- The hands reveal our basic level of sexual energy

and how it can be translated into passion, commitment, and our ability to love.

- They show our capacity for feeling, and can reveal mental and emotional blocks that inhibit its flow.
- The hands help us determine our level of compatibility with another, and how we can establish a relationship built on understanding and trust.
- By revealing traits, trends, and abilities that we may not be fully conscious of, the hand can help us change whatever blocks us from achieving satisfying relationships, enabling us to draw on our positive "core qualities," which we may have overlooked.

Although their significance can be modified by other aspects of the hand, two features closely associated with love, sex, and relationship include:

- the shape of the hand
- the shape of the fingertips

Hand Shapes

The Elementary Hand

The elementary hand is divided into two classifications: *lower elementary* and *higher elementary*.

Lower Elementary

The lower elementary hand is rarely found in its pure form. You can recognize it by its coarse, rough skin, strong stubby fingers, and stiff consistency.

The owner of this type of hand (usually a man) has a robust constitution, and great strength and endurance. He will have strong sexual drives and needs a partner who will satisfy those needs. When basic needs are satisfied—food, money, sex, and shelter—he will be happy. If these values are threatened, he can become violent, especially when drunk. Jealousy is a common trait.

The pure elementary type can be difficult to get along with. Yet with a strict, controlled upbringing he can be more "domesticated" and a hard worker and good bread-winner. Partners for this type include others with elementary hands, as well as those with strong hands that are somewhat squarish in form.

KEY PHRASES THAT DESCRIBE
OWNERS OF LOWER ELEMENTARY HANDS

- primitive, basic, crude
- often lacking in intelligent reasoning and imaginative understanding
- often selfish and short-sighted in relationships

Higher Elementary

The higher elementary type is far more common. Its basic shape may be the same as the lower elementary, but it is usually more flexible, revealing a more relaxed, responsive personality. Finer skin texture will increase sensitivity. The person is also likely to have a longer heart line (greater capacity for affection) and head line (more reasoning capacity).

KEY PHRASES THAT DESCRIBE
OWNERS OF HIGHER ELEMENTARY HANDS

- physically earthy, but gentle behind the tough exterior
- unlikely to be demonstrative
- represses feelings
- may need confidence boosted in relationship
- often creative, especially in carpentry, repairing things, cooking, working with animals or plants
- dependable and reliable provider and protector

The Square Hand

In the square hand, the palm, the fingernails, and the fingertips are squarish. And the owners of such hands are "square" indeed. Square-handed people tend to be conventional and strict observers of social customs. Life is a matter of routine, order, and system.

The same is true of their sex life. It tends to be the same day after day, for this is the way they prefer it—the same time, the same place, the same person, and the same way. The "square" person is loyal and seldom commits adultery.

KEY PHRASES THAT DESCRIBE
OWNERS OF LOWER ELEMENTARY HANDS

- controlled and restrained at the beginning of relationships
- sincere, honest, and direct when expressing affection
- often moralistic in their attitudes
- inflexible and disliking change
- usually punctual and reliable
- can be dull and unadventurous
- good workers and providers
- careful with money

The Spatulate Hand

The pure spatulate hand is rare, but it is also the easiest type to recognize. The broad fingertips resemble the spatula used in the kitchen. Owners of this type of hand are energetic and restless. They love action, excitement, and adventure, and cannot tolerate monotony and restrictions.

All this applies equally to their sexuality. If you are sexually inhibited or prefer predictable sexual encounters, and your partner has this type of hand, you are in trouble. He or she is likely to become bored with you and may commit adultery. However, such infidelities may have nothing to do with you or any inadequacy on your part, because it is in your partner's nature to seek new experiences. You must either tolerate and understand these needs or you will have to leave the relationship. If you choose to remain with a person with spatulate hands, keep yourself physically fit and attractive and learn new tricks as the years go by. Your partner is likely to keep coming back to you no matter how far he or she may stray.

KEY PHRASES THAT DESCRIBE OWNERS OF SPATULATE HANDS

- like variety and adventure in romance
- often irritable; strong critical tendencies
- may lack tidiness in personal appearance
- can get very involved in career or sports
- healthy sexual appetite

The Philosophic Hand

Though not a "pure" type that is part of our normal classification of hand shapes, the philosophic hand is easy to recognize because of its long palm and long, bony fingers with large joints and long nails (Figure 11.1). Owners of this hand have an analytical and inquiring mind. They will examine everything, try everything, and then form their own opinions. Convictions are acquired by this type of person through meditation and analysis. Such people are independent and do not depend on hearsay or non-authoritative statements. Whenever possible, they get the information firsthand.

Communication is the key to happiness with partners who possess this type of hand. Learn to talk with them about your

---

**KEY PHRASES THAT DESCRIBE
OWNERS OF PHILOSOPHIC HANDS**

- often complex and contradictory
- curious and interested in others
- not easily deceived; naturally skeptical
- retain individuality in relationships
- often very sensitive to criticism
- patient and considerate of others
- enjoy being alone

Figure 11.1: Philosophic hand

problems and your feelings, and be open to hearing from them as well. People with philosophic hands love to analyze, and it often takes them a long time to make decisions.

For this reason, they are rarely spontaneous, especially when it comes to sex and romance. While this can be frustrating (especially if you possess smooth, short fingers), becoming aware of this psychological trait can bring about greater understanding and compassion.

The Conic Hand

The conic hand is characterized by a triangular shape with tapering fingers. As opposed to square-handed individuals, people with conic hands tend to be impulsive, impatient, and sensitive. They respond to harmony, beauty, and artistic surroundings.

Their sex lives have sentimental and romantic overtones, and they will enjoy sex to the fullest only if the act is surrounded with mood-producing stimuli like music, perfume, and visual excitement, such as erotic clothing.

If your partner has this type of hand, you need to make it your business to create a mood that inspires love and excitement. Try not to become caught up in routine. Be spontaneous. Make everything you do seem romantic and appetizing.

**KEY PHRASES THAT DESCRIBE
OWNERS OF CONIC HANDS**

- emotional, intuitive, changeable
- idealistic, with high aspirations in relationships
- materialistic and opportunistic
- need constant stimulation; easily bored
- dislike routine and predictability in relationships
- can be reached on an emotional level
- love the unexpected compliment or gift
- sensuous, especially if hand consistency is thick

The Psychic Hand

Owners of the psychic hand (usually women) are highly sensitive, very idealistic in love, and appreciate all that is beautiful and refined. Aspirations are more spiritual and romantic than practical and down-to-earth.

People with psychic hands need to commit. They are often an inspiration to others and want to help them become better. However, they often place their partner on a pedestal, with frequent disillusionment. If your partner has this type of hand, be very sensitive to his or her needs and offer protection and support. Allow your partner to rely on you.

Sexual Energy

Energy moves the wheels of life. In humans, this energy is provided by the metabolic processes of the body. This has to do partly with the food we eat, the air we breathe, our own unique genetic makeup, and even our thoughts and attitudes.

Both the thickness and consistency of the hand indicate the amount of sexual energy we have at our disposal. However, other factors—including the size of the mount of Venus and the depth of the primary lines—can strengthen or neutralize these basic characteristics.

While hand thickness is somewhat determined by the individual's physique, the following observations apply:

Thin hands

- A very flat or soft hand reveals a low sex drive. The individual would tend to tire easily, would lack warmth, and would want to be "given to" rather than give in a relationship.

- A person with thin hands often lacks the warmth of the heart so necessary for a deep romantic attachment. The relationship may still be strong and lasting, but passion, romance, and sensuality may be lacking.

- If the hand is thin and hard, the person will be stubborn, inflexible and calculating. A strong withholding current would be a major identifying trait.

Thick hands

A thick hand reveals the opposite qualities: an abundance of warmth, energy, and sensuality.

- *Thick and soft:* Love for food and drink in addition to sex. Setting limits on these pleasures can be difficult, and weight control is often a problem.

- *Hard and inflexible:* Accentuates a stubborn, cold, and unbending emotional quality. People with this type of hand tend to be sexually aggressive, emotionally demanding, and difficult to be with. They think mostly about their own pleasure, especially if their heart line is short or free from islands and branches.

- *Thick with elastic consistency:* Warm and sensuous individual with an abundance of sexual energy. This type of person enjoys a balance between receiving and giving pleasure, and generally finds it easy to establish and maintain good relationships.

- *Medium thickness:* Energetic, warm people. Like their attitude towards food and drink, their sexual key-word is *balance.* While they are not often celibate or disinterested in sex, it does not normally occupy all (or even most) of their thoughts and energy.

The Mount of Venus

The mount of Venus represents the natural driving forces and the instinctive potential of an individual. It is also a primary indicator of passion and sex drive. It speaks of vitality, the capacity for friendship, and our ability to love.

Ideally, this mount should take up about one-third of the palm, outlined by a widely sweeping life line. It should be neither too hard nor too bland. "Nice and round" would best describe a good mount of Venus. If the mount of Venus is of average elevation and does not have deep lines running across it, the person will be warm, lovable, and interested in sex. This type of mount will also indicate a love of beauty.

- *Very large:* Often an excess of physical passion and sexuality.

- *Hard and very large:* Sexual aggression, brutality, and cruelty (especially if the mount is reddish in color and the upper mount of Mars is pronounced).

- *Strong grilles:* Accentuate physical passion and sexual interest, even to the point of being obsessive.

- *Small and bland mount:* General lack of vitality and sexual power. Although the person may well have strong feelings of love and passion, they are not expressed primarily through sex and physical contact.

- *Life line cutting through mount:* Cold and prudish temperament. Sexual expression is not a priority.

Skin Texture and Sex

The texture of the skin is another important factor in determining psychosexual makeup.

- *Smooth, fine skin:* A strong degree of sensitivity and impressionability. Sex and sexual relations are often elevated to a romantic, idealized level. The person is more likely to respond to imagery and fantasy in sexual situations, and can easily be affected by the energy, thoughts, and words of the partner.

- *Coarse skin texture:* Less sensitive nature. Person

tends to respond more to purely physical drives and stimuli, especially if a physical heart line is present in the hands. The individual is more prone to lack tact and sensitivity in sexual situations, and may not always be receptive to the partner's needs.

When a man has a thick hand with coarse skin texture and his mate has a hand that is primarily thin and fine, chances are good that their relationship will be neither sexually nor emotionally compatible. However, by becoming aware of the differences in their hands and sexual personalities, each partner could work on becoming more understanding of the other's sexual and emotional needs, and can strengthen their relationship as a result.

- *Medium skin texture:* High degree of sensitivity and a balance between the receptive and active principles. While open to impressions and responsive to the feelings and needs of their partner, individuals with medium skin texture are also able to assert themselves in relationships in a healthy way.

Flexibility

The flexibility of the hand in general and the thumb in particular can also tell us much about the way we respond to others in relationships.

- *Hard, inflexible:* Stubborn, rigid personality. These people are set in their ways and have difficulty accepting new ideas and adapting to unfamiliar situations.

- *Plus stiff thumb:* Sign of material and emotional stinginess. On the positive side, however, a person with a rigid hand and thumb would be reliable and emotionally stable. If you had a date with such an individual, he or she would be sure to meet you at the appointed place exactly on time!

- *Flexible:* The more flexible the hand, the greater the ability to adapt. There is an increased capacity to be open to new ideas and to flow with new situations. The ability to adapt is essential to a successful relationship, and people with flexible hands do it well. They are often more amenable to sharing their problems in a relationship, and also more approachable and less defensive than people with stiff hands. By the same token, they are frequently less predictable. The person with flexible hands will probably not arrive on time for a date, despite the best of intentions. When the owner of a flexible hand has a thumb that bends back easily, generosity—both with material objects and feelings—is strong.

- *Extremely flexible hands*: Extremely flexible hands easily bend back to a ninety-degree angle or more.

People with this type of hand can be very exciting in a relationship. They are known for their spontaneity, adaptability, and generosity, and can often be unpredictable and temperamental. However, if the thumb is weak and supple and the heart line is long and chained, sentiments can easily shift, and a committed monogamous relationship is often difficult to maintain.

The Fingers and Sex

The Thumb

The angle that the thumb forms with the rest of the hand is a good indication of the existence or lack of sexual inhibition. Be sure to compare both hands to determine whether the individual has become more sexually liberated with age, or if sexual inhibitions have increased over the years.

- *High-set:* A high-set thumb, opening at a forty-five degree angle to the index finger, is a sign of a Victorian in sexual attitudes. These individuals are overly careful, correct, and withdrawn. They are either embarrassed about sexual matters or avoid them completely.

- *Medium-set:* When the thumb is at a sixty-degree angle, there is a greater degree of psychological openness. While the person is more liberated than the Victorian, there is still a fear of "letting go," especially if the hand is stiff and the head and life lines are joined.

- *Low-set*: As the angle of the thumb increases, there is a corresponding lack of sexual inhibition. When the angle of the thumb in its relation to the index finger exceeds ninety degrees, the individual tends to be sexually integrated and self-accepting. Sexual repression and fear of experimentation are minimal, especially if the hands are flexible. When there is a separation between the lines of life and head as well, these people have strong feelings of self-confidence and independence, which will carry over into their relationships.

Finger Shapes

In addition to the thumb, the other fingers of the hand can tell us much about the way we relate to others. If the fingers are slender and pointed at the tips, there is often a lack of control over instinctive desires. If this trait is coupled with a supple thumb and a long, chained heart line, there may be difficulties maintaining a love relationship with one person.

Fingers that are more squared-off or rounded at the tip can indicate a more monogamous trend in relationships, but should not be seen as a guarantee of faithfulness.

A strong thumb points towards relationships that are stable and constant. However, be sure to consider all of the characteristics of the hand together before reaching conclusions!

Jupiter

Ideally, the Jupiter and Apollo fingers should be the same length, and measure approximately one-quarter inch (.6cm) shorter than the Saturn finger. Such a configuration indicates that there is a good level of self-esteem plus the ability to appreciate the give-and-take aspects of a relationship.

When the Jupiter finger is shorter than Apollo, there is often a lack of self-esteem, which can lead to self-denigration and not standing up for one's rights. When the life and head lines are joined, there is often a concern over what "others" may think about one's beliefs or conduct. This tendency can be modified by a separation between the life and head lines at their commencement.

When the Jupiter finger is longer than Apollo, the individual tends to be prideful and vain, and often needs to be the dominant one in the relationship. The psychological need for sexual conquests is common. When the life and head lines are connected, there is often a fear that "If I'm not in charge, someone will control me." When the life and head lines are separate, there is a greater degree of independence and impulsiveness. While the person may be domineering and like to be in charge, this trait is not based on fear, but is merely an aspect of leadership ability.

A straight Jupiter finger displays the finest Jupiterian qualities: generosity, leadership, and warmth. To the degree that this finger bends towards Saturn, we have a person who is insecure, jealous, or possessive. When the Mercury finger bends in as well, there can be the tendency to do "whatever is necessary" in a relationship to get his or her way.

Saturn

When the Saturn finger bends slightly towards Apollo, the individual enjoys solitude and often needs space in a relationship. This shouldn't be interpreted as being anti-social or withholding—the person merely needs to spend time alone.

If the finger bends sharply towards Apollo, however, the tendency towards melancholy and depression are more pronounced. If the space between the head line and heart line is narrow, the individual can be secretive as well. People with such hands need to be with friends who are both trustworthy and understanding, and who can patiently help them to slowly open up and share their problems and feelings.

Apollo

When the Apollo finger is straight, the individual is a good judge of character. However, when this finger bends towards Saturn, there is a tendency to place others on a pedestal and not see them as they really are. This can lead to disillusionment in relationships, because these people expect more from others than can realistically be given.

Mercury

An ideal sex partner must know how to do more than make love artfully: He or she must also know how to communicate. A long Mercury finger highlights the capacity to communicate and relate well to others romantically. Some palmists believe that this finger is the most important guidepost to the capacity to establish and maintain satisfying romantic and sexual relationships.

Generally speaking, the longer the Mercury finger, the greater the ability to communicate and relate to others. An ideal Mercury finger should reach the top phalange of the ring or Apollo finger, while a "long" Mercury finger would reach well into the top phalange of the Apollo finger,

(Figure 11.2). Because the Mercury finger is often set lower in the hand than the others, take the Mercury finger of one hand and place it on the Apollo finger of the other in order to gauge its actual length.

Perhaps the greatest advantage of those having a long little finger is their ability to communicate their feelings to their partner, as well as articulate their love. These people are excellent conversationalists, often diplomatic, and have the ability to charm their partners and convince them of their love.

Figure 11.2: Long Mercury finger

When this finger is short—reaching one-quarter inch (.6cm) below the joint between the second and top phalange of the Apollo finger—interpersonal communication and satisfying sexual relations can be difficult.

Aside from length, a very low-set Mercury finger (Figure 11.3) is said to reveal that sexual matters are the major keynote of the person's life.

When the Mercury finger is straight, it reveals a basically

Figure 11.3: Short, low-set Mercury finger

honest and straightforward individual. He or she may also lack shrewdness and diplomacy, except where a waisted thumb phalange is present. Very often this person is taken advantage of by others and regarded as gullible and naive. These qualities are accentuated in the rare cases where the Mercury finger actually bends outward, away from the hand.

When this finger bends inwards slightly in the direction of the ring finger, there is a tendency towards shrewdness and diplomacy. The greater the curve towards Apollo, the greater the tendency to be manipulative and dishonest. Many successful used car salespeople and politicians have a long, curving Mercury finger.

When the space between the Mercury and Apollo fingers is noticeably wider than that between the other fingers, the individual is an independent, often unconventional thinker. Such people are often out of the mainstream of sexual philosophy and practice, and do not conform to the established standards of society. As a result, they are prone to experience isolation and frustration in their romantic and sexual life.

Nails

The nails are also helpful in determining character and how we relate to others.

- *Long, broad and slightly rounded:* Openness, broad-mindedness, generosity, and a non-critical nature.

- *Long, narrow:* Suspicion, selfishness, and a tendency to be shrewd and calculating in relationships.
- *Short:* Critical individuals who not only focus on the perceived shortcomings of others, but are also very self-critical. They often sabotage and downplay their personal talents and positive character traits, which instead deserve recognition and expression.

Nail color is also an expression of sexual vitality.

- *Reddish:* Strong sex drive. Owners are more able to express their passion in purely physical terms.
- *Bright pink:* Modifies this powerful sex drive. Owners tend to enjoy a balance between physical and emotional expressions of love and passion.
- *Bluish:* Difficulty expressing oneself physically. Although they may not lack passion and strong love feelings, it often takes them some time to "warm up" to someone in a relationship.

Lines

Heart Line

Of all the lines in the hand, the heart line is the primary indicator of the way we feel towards others and how we relate to them. In addition, it reveals both the strength and type of our sexual expression.

The palmists of India consider the heart line to be paramount, and, unless this line is satisfactory, there is no need to study the palm further. This makes it easy to understand why love and sex is such an important factor in life to the Hindus, as shown by their literature and the erotic nature of their temple decorations. They not only believe that sex creates life but also that sex prolongs it. Perhaps this is why the palmists of India call the line of the heart the line of life. Here are some basic meanings of different types of heart line formations:

- *Long, deep, smooth; free of islands and breaks:* Indicator of strong feelings of affection, balanced by reliable and constant emotions. People with this kind of heart line tend to feel secure in love and are devoted to their partner.

- *Deep and chained:* High sensitivity. These individuals often feel vulnerable in a relationship. There is a strong desire for intimate contact, yet an equally strong fear of commitment. Such individuals need to be honest with feelings and try to lower psychological defenses. Otherwise, they can be taken for being aloof and disinterested, when in reality the opposite may be true.

- *Chained and islanded:* Inconsistency in feelings, with

the emotions often confused and fragmented. When the heart line is wavy as well, these traits are often more pronounced.

- *Straight (Figure 11.4)*: Sensitive and "mental" personality. Fantasies, romantic imagery, and receptivity to emotional stimuli often predominate. This heart line is sometimes referred to as "feminine" by palmists, because strong emotions and receptivity are commonly considered feminine characteristics. However, this type of heart line is found on both women and men and should be more accurately termed a "mental/receptive" heart line. People with this type of line—especially when it ends at or near the Jupiter mount—are more likely to be guided by

Figure 11.4: Straight heart line

romantic feelings than common sense, and are also more likely to be in love with humanity as a whole than romantically committed to a single individual. Perhaps this is why such a line is also known as a "humanitarian heart line."

- *Curved (Figure 11.5)*: More physical than mental, and more assertive than receptive, a person with this type of heart line is more likely to be influenced by purely physical stimuli and instincts. Sexual expression will probably be more physical, active, and assertive.

- *Ending under Saturn:* The person may be quite physical, but on a deep level is ruled more by reason than by feelings. In general, sexual impulses are strong

Figure 11.5: Curved heart line

(especially if the mount of Venus is large and the heart line is "physical" in character, as discussed on the previous pages). If the heart line is strong and clear with a minimum of branches, individuals may need to develop greater sensitivity to their partner's needs, although a small fork or branch at the end of the line adds a degree of receptivity to the personality.

- *Ending between Saturn and Jupiter:* Healthy balance between the heart and the head, or between reason and emotion. While the person would tend to be warm-hearted, generous, and sympathetic to others, there is also emotional balance and objectivity.

- *Ending under Jupiter:* Emotions tend to predominate over reason. Idealized love, sentimentality, and a strong degree of loyalty are common traits of those with this type of heart line. The tendency towards possessiveness and jealousy is often accentuated, especially if the Jupiter finger bends towards Saturn.

- *Moving clear across palm; drops to touch head and life lines:* Often strong conflict between the heart and the head, which can lead to much suffering. If the heart line is chained (and it usually is), these people have experienced a difficult childhood and are very easily hurt. Such feelings are often intensified by a strong girdle of Venus. Individuals are often romantically attracted to numerous people and have trouble reconciling their universal affections with what society expects of them. On the positive side, they are compassionate and sensitive to others, and can easily identify with those who suffer and who are in need. For this reason, many people with this type of heart line make excellent healers, teachers, therapists, ministers, and others who like to help people.

- *Wide space between heart and head lines:* Broad-mindedness and an unconventional mental outlook, especially if there is a wide separation between the Apollo and Mercury fingers.

- *Narrow space between heart and head lines:* Strong degree of secrecy and a feeling of not being "at home" in the world. People with this formation often have difficulty expressing their feelings and are frequently self-conscious in social situations.

- *Branches at end of heart line:* These add to the individual's sensitivity and receptivity.

- *Heart line ending in three short branches:* Balance between sentiment, passion, and common sense.

Head Line

The direction of the head line also needs to be taken into account when considering sex and relationship in the hand.

- *Head line moving directly across palm:* Realistic view of love and relationship. The person is often conventional, proper, and practical, where romance is concerned.

- *Head line drooping towards Luna mount:* The more the head line droops towards the mount of Luna, the greater the imagination and fantasy life. Since these qualities can be either positive or negative, depending on other character traits, be sure to look for confirming or modifying factors in the hand (with special attention to the fingers and their shape) before arriving at any conclusions.

Hint: A good way to interpret the significance of the heart and head lines is to compare the two. When the heart line is more pronounced than the head line, the urge for affection and love will outweigh most other interests. When the head line is stronger and more pronounced, the love nature will be governed more by the mind. Intellectual companionship is often preferred to sexual companionship.

Saturn Line

The degree of adaptation that a person is able to make in relationships is indicated by the start of the fate line, the vertical line in the center of the palm.

If the fate line begins inside the life line or is closely attached to the life line (Figure 11.6), the individual was greatly influenced by the parent of the opposite sex and will likely transfer these needs, good or bad, to the partner. If such a hand belongs to a woman, her partner would do well to treat her just as a kindly, affectionate father might treat a favored and much-loved daughter. If this configuration is seen on the man's hand, his partner must come to understand his need to be nurtured without being smothered. If the fate line starts in the center of the palm, independent of the life line, the individual (whether a male or female) will tend to be psychologically independent of the partner. Such individuals demand to be an equal partner in the relationship.

When the fate line rises from the mount of Luna, the individuals are likely to be greatly influenced by their mate. They are the type who will always love, honor, and cherish, but the partner must deserve their devotion and respect their submissive nature. This submissive tendency will be strengthened if the index

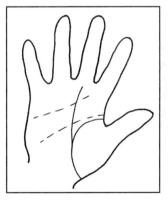

Figure 11.6: Fate line joined to life line

finger is short and the life and head lines are joined at their commencement.

If the fate line stops short of the head line after rising from the mount of Luna, individuals will tend to be submissive. They will likely worship their partner and are likely to accept every demand and imposition.

Individuals who lack a fate line tend to be unpredictable. Ideally, their partner should have a strong fate line and a strong ego to help complement and guide their impulsive nature. Trouble awaits a couple who both have faulty fate lines or no fate lines at all. If both have strong fate lines, both have the willpower to bring harmony to the relationship.

Like the other lines of the hand, the Saturn line has the ability to change according to our individual attitudes and actions. Each of us has a specific task or tasks in life and a goal to accomplish.

Girdle of Venus

When considering the heart and head lines, we should also evaluate the meaning of the so-called Girdle of Venus. A semicircular crease line located above the heart line, it usually runs between the base of the index and fourth fingers (Figures 11.7 and 11.8). When found on the hand, it is sometimes regarded as an adjunct to the heart line.

Figure 11.7: Clear and well-formed Girdle of Venus

Figure 11.8: Chained and poorly formed Girdle of Venus

Tradition links the Girdle of Venus with strong sexual appetites, especially if it is complemented by a large mount of Venus. Generally speaking, a girdle reveals a high level of emotional response. Its owners are easily impressed by suggestion and sexual imagery, although the degree of response depends on the clarity, length, and depth of the line itself, in addition to that of the heart and head lines.

- A short and clear Girdle of Venus (Figure 11.7) is a good sign of emotional alertness. It is usually found in professional entertainers, musicians, artists, and others known to be easily moved emotionally, and reveals a sense of balance in one's emotions and sexuality.

- A long and broken girdle (Figure 11.8) can be a difficult sign, as it reveals people who may have trouble finding fulfillment for their emotional needs. It can also reveal difficulty in releasing emotional tension. It is common in individuals who are extremely sensitive and given to temper tantrums because they have not found ways to release their pent-up nervous energies.

During the last century, when "hysteria" was prevalent, the Girdle of Venus was called by palmists "the line of hysteria." Today we may consider it the symbol of frustrated individuals who are unsuccessfully searching for release from their energies in sexual activities. Because this sexual energy is present in both those with hysteria and those with a tendency towards sexual promiscuity, it can also be called "the line of the libido."

The Hand and Sexual Preference

It is difficult to determine sexual preference from one or two aspects of the hand, because sexuality is an expression of the *whole person* and how he or she relates to life. Sexuality has its roots in our basic genetic makeup, our educational and cultural conditioning, and especially our primary relationships with our mother and father. Each sexual relationship mobilizes different aspects of this reality in us. For this reason, it is important to consider sexuality as part of the overall personality rather than as a separate part of one's life.

Gay or Straight?

Nearly every book on palmistry has added to the confusion that exists regarding same-sex orientation. The hand of a homosexual—invariably a male—has been portrayed as weak, with a supple thumb (indicating an unstable personality and lack of will power), a broken or islanded head line (indicating emotional problems), a long, chained heart line (showing that emotions rule over reason), a long, broken Girdle of Venus (indicating sensitivity and a strong sexual appetite), and pointy fingers (revealing artistic tendencies, capriciousness, and lack of emotional balance).

It is very difficult—if not impossible—to determine sexual preference from the hand. People with same-sex orientation are found in every culture and profession, and represent a wide spectrum of personality traits and human emotions. Psychologists have found that in almost every area but sexual orientation, "straight" and "gay" people are identical. Some gay people have problems with self-esteem while others do not; some are sensitive while others are not; some are socially well-adjusted while others are not. While certain gay men enjoy flower arranging, some prefer rugby, while others like both flower arranging *and* rugby.

In many cases, the boundaries between homosexual, bisexual, and heterosexual expression are quite vague, and blanket statements rarely serve a worthwhile purpose.

The hand can, of course, provide insight into the person's sensitivity, emotional response, the degree of sexual repression that operates in the personality, issues of aggression and passivity, cruelty, the capacity for love, and the ability to enjoy fulfilling relationships. Whether such feelings are directed primarily towards men or women (or both) is extremely difficult to assess.

Other avenues of sexual expression—including sado-masochism, incest, voyeurism, and fetishes—are often caused by energetic blocks on both physical and psychological levels, and are difficult to determine by hand analysis alone.

Like sexual preference, the boundary between having such inclinations and acting them out is often very fine. Psychologists tell us that nearly everyone has entertained thoughts of sadism, masochism, incest, or voyeurism at one time or another, even though such feelings are rarely, if ever, expressed.

It is vital that we avoid stereotyping hands. A "sadist's hand," for example, is supposed to be coarse, hard, and red in color. We have been told that the mounts of Venus and Mars should be large and hard, and a "Murderer's thumb" is often present. The problem is that there are people with such hands who are not sadists, while some people with fine hands, long, slim fingers, and fine skin texture may act out their sadistic feelings every day of the week. Again, it is important to view the hand as a *totality* and to be open to intuitive perceptions rather than stereotypes.

Marriage in the Hand

The so-called "marriage lines" of the hand (Figure 11.9) are actually lines of union. They indicate the potential—and possible time frame—of an important relationship (or relationships) in a person's life.

As discussed previously, this union may be with a man or a woman and may or may not include sex. In some cases, as in the hands of people for whom legal marriage is superficial or

Figure 11.9: Union lines

psychologically distant, the line of union can indicate a close friend with whom there is a primary, though not necessarily sexual, relationship.

How can we know as to whether a line of union indicates a traditional marriage or not? As with other major aspects of the hand, the reader's intuition can play a major role in evaluating the present and potential existence of a marriage-quality relationship.

- In general, the longer the line of union, the longer the relationship.

- The deeper the line, the more important the relationship is in the person's life.

- Breaks or islands indicate problems in the relationship that can lead to its termination.

- A branch at the end of the union line means that the partners may gradually drift apart.

- When the union line drops slightly towards the end, it is believed that the person will probably outlive the mate.

Note that, of all the lines of the hand, the union lines are the most likely to change: branches disappear, breaks can mend, and the line can get longer or shorter in a matter of months. These changes reflect different attitudes and circumstances in the person's life. For that reason, statements like "This island shows that your marriage will end" may be both incorrect and potentially harmful to the people concerned.

Compatibility

In addition to providing important insights regarding a couple's ability to relate to each other, modern palmistry can also answer important questions concerning compatibility: Is one of the partners undersexed or oversexed? Which partner is dominant and which is more dependent and submissive?

Marks of Sensuality

From the mount of Venus and the shape of the little finger we can determine the sensuality of an individual. As stated earlier, if the mount of Venus is well developed and the little finger is long, we probably have a sensual person who loves physical contact, affection, and sex.

If the mount of Venus is flat, the little finger short, and the consistency of the hand weak, chances are that sex will not play an important role in the person's life. If both partners have this type of hand, they will likely be compatible with each other. If other features of the hand are complementary, the keynote of their relationship would be likely to include mutual respect, intellectual compatibility, and shared interests, such as books, art, or theater. However, their sexual connection would probably not be a primary aspect of their relationship.

Sexual compatibility is a major component of a harmonious, enduring relationship. If the hands of both partners reveal a similar degree of sensuality, they have a good chance at making the relationship a success. However if one partner is very sensual and the other is not, conflicts are likely to plague the relationship. One partner will feel sexually frustrated, while the other will feel that he or she is being imposed upon.

Marks of Domination

A well-developed, long index finger with an enlarged muscular pattern at the base signifies a dominating nature. Such people like to be in charge, in control. They enjoy being "on top" in their relationships.

If both partners are sensual or if both are not, no problem is likely to arise. Unless other major difficulties are present in the relationship, a woman with a low sex drive is not likely leave a husband who is not sexually demanding, nor will a highly sexed woman leave a man who is ready for lovemaking at any time.

However important sex may be, often it becomes secondary in a compatible marriage where one partner is dominant and the other submissive or dependent by nature. Couples seldom engage in adultery or get divorced when one who has to dominate in order to be happy chooses a partner who likes to be dominated. The best results are obtained when one partner is as dominant as the other is submissive.

Impotence and Frigidity

On the subject of compatibility, we need to understand that there are physical, energetic, and psychological causes of impotence and frigidity. While there are no clear-cut indications of these sexual problems on the hand, we can observe several features that may contribute to the problem.

- A small or weak mount of Venus, a thin hand of flabby consistency, a life line cutting through the mount of Venus, and a weak heart line can indicate that sexual expression is not a major priority in life.

However, other factors should be considered. While the hand markings mentioned above may reveal potential, the actual relationship between the two people involved is of primary importance. Before we consider an individual problem, we need to see it in the light of that specific relationship and the conscious or unconscious energetic connection between the partners. If, however the difficulty were chronic—for example, if the man had been impotent in his four previous relationships as well—it would be an individual problem to be worked with accordingly.

12

CAREER AND
SELF-FULFILLMENT

Ideally, our career should be more than just a job, or an activity that serves only our basic survival needs. It should also be a *vocation*, or an activity that provides a sense of self-fulfillment, self-worth, or contribution to society. While it need not occupy all of our talent, time, and energy, a career should be conducive to our personal, professional, and spiritual well-being. It should provide pleasure, challenge, and opportunities for personal growth.

Because the lines can always change, the hand can offer us continuing guidance regarding career direction and personal fulfillment. By getting in touch with our deepest aspirations, talents, and skills, we can begin to attract people, circumstances, and opportunities that open the door to satisfying and purposeful careers.

The basic hand types reveal certain core qualities that enable us to achieve fulfillment in life. At the same time, a basic quality may also point to the need to develop a complementary or "shadow" quality, in order to obtain a greater level of personal integration and satisfaction.

This is especially true when our career path appears stale or chronically frustrating. For example, for an accountant whose squarish hands, squarish fingertips, and knotty fingers indicate organizing ability and an interest in detail and analysis, a possible career alternative may involve working with the theater, the arts, or in an area where he can integrate complementary qualities such as intuition, spontaneity, or emotion into his work life. This may not necessarily involve a complete career change (from accountant to movie star), but rather a career *modification* that could include serving as a financial manager or consultant for a dance company, or taking up acting or singing purely as an avocation. Again, the point to remember is: If the person is happy with life, there is no problem. But if there is an overriding sense of restlessness or frustration, the other side of the personality may need to be developed and expressed.

There is no rigid standard for success in one's career. While the passive hand reveals our talents and possibilities, our dominant hand indicates the degree to which we are utilizing these capacities at the moment.

First, the Modifiers

Before we explore specific hand types, mounts, and major lines in reference to career choice, let us first note several important modifying factors.

- To the degree that the thumb is set high, low, or medium, we can determine the level of self-confidence and independence. It will also indicate whether or not the temperament is introverted or extroverted.

- The size and shape of the thumb can show the degree of ego strength, leadership, and will power and reveal how they relate to career choice and performance on the job.

- When the life and head lines separate, the individual tends to be impulsive, impatient, and self-reliant. The further the lines are apart, the greater the self-confidence and extroversion.

- When the life and head lines connect at their commencement, the individual tends to be introverted, careful, and may lack self-confidence and self-esteem. The longer these lines run together, the more cautious and introverted the personality, especially if the thumb is set high on the hand.

- The greater the flexibility of the hand, the more adaptable and flexible the personality. People with extremely flexible hands tend to lack emotional stability, especially if confirming factors are present in the hand.

- Finely textured skin reflects a sensitive nature, while coarse skin is found on people who are more "rough and tumble." A man with a strong hand with fine skin may be drawn to a white collar job like business administration, while his counterpart with coarsely textured skin would prefer being the foreman on a construction site or the manager of a business selling replacement parts for automobiles.

Loops

- The presence of a loop of seriousness reveals an ambitious and earnest individual, whose professional goals primarily include money, responsibility, and advancement. This loop is often found on business people, scientists, and others who have a fundamentally serious approach to life and work.

- A loop of humor reveals more light-hearted individuals whose primary goals include an interesting job and a stimulating and pleasurable work environment. Although they may earn lots of money, it is not their primary goal.

Fingerprints

- Arches on the fingerprints reveal a practical side to the personality.
- Whorls indicate a person who is more original, complex, and temperamental.
- Loops reveal a middle-of-the-road personality who has the ability to adapt and fit into different work situations.

Hand Types and Career Choice

Elementary Hands

Elementary hands are useful hands. People with these hands tend to be slow, careful, and practical. They see the "bottom line" or the essence of things, and they often like to work with their hands. They include farmers, mechanics, people who work with heavy machinery, and those who do work involving strong physical labor. They often enjoy the slower pace of country life, and frequently reflect the simpler, down-to-earth feeling that rural life provides.

Square Hands

Like elementary hands, square hands are useful hands. They reveal the ability to organize, persevere, and get things done. Order, stability, and common sense are among the major qualities of the squarish hand, which make for precision, thoroughness, and a systematic approach in dealing with ideas and projects.

Work-related key phrases regarding elementary-handed people include:

- suspicious of new ideas and technologies; like the "tried and true"
- do not like to change jobs
- emotions develop slowly and deeply
- will complete assignments
- love hard work

Although skin texture, predominant fingers, and certain lines can modify the major attributes of the square hand, it is often found in executives, organizers, and politicians. Square hands are also common among administrative assistants, clerks, and secretaries who have the ability to organize an office or business. Computer programmers and operators (especially if the fingers are knotted) are favored by squarish hands, as are teachers (especially those who specialize in geometry and languages), engineers, lawyers, doctors, librarians, and accountants. Landscape architecture and interior design are possible career choices as well, especially if the head line reveals a good imagination.

Key work-related phrases to describe people with squarish hands include:

- well organized and reliable
- liking to follow rules and established procedures

- looking for connections between things and wanting to know how isolated parts fit together into the whole picture
- emotionally stable and able to deal with stress

Spatulate Hands

People with spatulate hands tend to be exciting and extroverted. Their firm yet flexible hands often reveal distinctive spatulate-tipped fingers and a round, strong palm.

Like those with squarish hands, people with spatulate hands make good executives, although their strength is geared more towards leadership than administration. They make excellent entrepreneurs, business people, managers, and inventors. When healing ability is present, small vertical lines or Samaritan lines on the mount of Mercury are a major sign of healing power.

People with spaulate hands are often attracted to jobs

CHARACTERISTIC OF SPATULATE HANDS

- strong, clear lines revealing energy and intensity
- fingers short when compared to the palm
- whorl fingerprints most common

---

that offer challenge, adventure, and change. Careers in business, law enforcement, fire protection, health, the creative arts (such as dance, crafts, and design), as well as skilled manual trades (such as plumbing and carpentry) are common professions for people with spatulate hands.

Some key work-related phrases that describe people with spatulate hands are:

- extroverted personality
- active; don't like to follow routine
- like to be in charge and control situations
- best suited for careers involving excitement, adventure, and innovation

Conic Hands

Conic hands reveal an individual who is sensitive, creative, and thoughtful.

Women with conic hands tend to gravitate towards the classic "feminine" occupations, like modeling, hairdressing, office work, and retail sales involving beauty and style, such as clothing or home furnishings.

A small number of men have conic hands. They are often attracted to low-pressure jobs in retail sales, working in a library, and office work, such as computer programming or word processing.

CHARACTERISTICS OF CONIC HANDS

- rounded palm with smooth, tapering fingers
- usually many fine lines in addition to the major lines
- soft skin consistency with flexible thumbs and fingers
- whorl prints most common

Key phrases to describe conic-handed people at work include:

- a liking for professions where they can express innate sensitivity and good taste
- thoughtful and studious
- easily influenced by other people and outer circumstances
- making decisions based on hunches and intuition

Psychic Hands

People with psychic hands would be drawn to many of the same careers as those with conic hands.

Finger Shapes and Career Direction

Squarish

People with squarish fingertips are most often organized and practical. They are apt to be thorough, systematic, and to have the ability to get things done. Many executives, organizers, clerks, administrative assistants, and secretaries have squarish fingers, as well as members of other professions who take an organized, systematic approach to their work.

Spatulate

Spatulate fingertips reveal action. People with spatulate fingertips predominating have the ability to seize the moment and use it in a practical way. Business executives, entrepreneurs, managers, and athletes may have spatulate fingers.

Conic

Conic fingertips reveal creativity. They reflect a love of beauty and an ability to beautify one's surroundings. Governed by inspiration rather than reason, people with conic-predominant fingertips are often imaginative and idealistic in their work environment.

Round

Round fingertips are the most common, reflecting a well-rounded and capable individual who may gravitate towards a variety of professions. Check other features of the hand for more specific information.

Most hands will reflect more than one of the fingertip shapes just described. Chances are that they will reveal a combination of attributes. In that case, it is important to pay special attention to each finger and evaluate how its qualities can influence career choice. If the Apollo finger is spatulate, for example, it can indicate a talent for public speaking, teaching, or acting. If the Jupiter finger is squarish, it reveals strong administrative ability. By taking account of these two traits alone, a possible career in public relations, politics, or business would be indicated.

The Mounts

Jupiter

A strong Jupiter mount indicates leadership. While politics, religious leadership, and business administration are viewed as standard career directions, people with a prominent Jupiter mount often find satisfaction in running a business, school, or other organization, and are drawn to counseling, teaching, and working with nature and animals. In general, however, people with strong Jupiter mounts prefer to be in a position of authority and independence on the job and often have difficulty working for others. For this reason, many are self-employed.

Saturn

Saturn is considered the mount of balance, and reflects such qualities as wisdom, sobriety, and responsibility. Unlike the Jupiterian, who is more sociable and outgoing, the pure Saturn type prefers to work alone. For people with coarsely-textured hands, work in agriculture, construction, and environmental protection are possible career choices. For others, mathematics (both teaching and research), engineering, physics, environmental science, and computer technology might be of career interest.

A strong Saturn mount also favors philosophical and religious studies, writing (especially on scientific themes), clerical work, library science, antique or building restoration, research of all kinds, and detailed work in arts, crafts, and design, especially if the fingers are knotted.

Apollo

A strong mount of Apollo is a sign of artistic flair, a sense of style and brilliance. Professions related to the performing arts, advertising, public relations, and sales are indicated by a strong Apollo mount and finger, as are careers in applied and fine arts (including architecture, design, painting, sculpture, landscaping, and graphic arts), especially if a whorl is present on the Apollo finger.

If this configuration is enhanced by a long and prominent Mercury finger (Figure 12.1), the ability to communicate is strengthened.

Other career possibilities for an Apollonian include teaching (especially where lecturing is involved), art and music therapy, and any job involving public contact such as receptionist, secretary, beautician, social worker, or psychotherapist.

Mercury

Mercury is the mount of business and communication. People with a prominent mount of Mercury are known for their ability to relate well to others. Careers in business, banking, sales, and related fields are popular among people with a strong Mercury mount and finger, while journalism, law, teaching, broadcasting, the natural sciences, and language arts are other possible career directions.

When Samaritan lines are present—as in the hand of the registered nurse shown in Figure 12.2—a career in the health care field (including medicine, laboratory technology,

Figure 12.1: Handprint with whorl on Apollo finger and a long Mercury finger

Figure 12.2: Handprint showing Samaritan lines

psychology, chiropractic, osteopathy, homeopathy, massage therapy, dentistry, or spiritual healing) is favored.

Mars

A strong mount of upper Mars, which is located under the mount of Mercury, reveals courage and resistance, with the

ndprint showing small, fine lines moving diago-
ount of Luna

armth, kindness, and humanity to the power
ounts.

ong mount of Saturn, which favors isolation, a
unt of Venus encourages personal involvement

ability to remain calm in the face of danger. Traditionally, hand readers have advised that people with strong mounts of Mars join the military services or police force, or take up professional boxing or wrestling as a career.

Although these stereotyped ideas may have some validity (people with a strong mount of upper Mars *are* often drawn to military service and law enforcement), other career possibilities should be considered as well.

Men and women with strong mounts of Mars have a talent for working with three-dimensional reality. They love challenge and revel in accomplishment. Careers involving athletics, dance, and physical fitness, the building trades (including carpentry, masonry, and plumbing), mechanics (involving automobiles, business machines, or household appliances), manual labor, agriculture, and environmental protection are possible areas of career interest, especially if the hand is of the elementary, spatulate, or mixed type. Recently I read the hand of an elegant woman who had an unusually strong mount of upper Mars. She was the CEO of a large company that provided security guards for businesses and sports events.

A large lower mount of Mars, located between the thumb and index finger, can be found on all kinds of hands, and reveals a strong assertive quality to the personality. An executive with a prominent mount of lower Mars, a strong thumb, and a loop of seriousness has a good chance of making it to the top of the professional ladder.

Luna

The lunar mount symbolizes imagination, instinct, and intuition. A strong mount also reveals our protective, nurturing feelings towards friends and family, as well as a love of travel.

When the mount of Luna is well developed (especially when accompanied by Samaritan lines on the mount of Mercury), a career in the helping professions—such as counseling, health care, social work, or teaching—might be indicated. Pilots, flight attendants, butlers, chauffeurs, travel agents, and tour coordinators often possess strong mounts of Luna, especially when they have a life line (or tiny lines branching off the life line) moving in the direction of the Luna mount (Figure 12.3). The presence of these lines often indicate a love for travel.

A prominent Luna mount also enhances the imagination, and is frequently found on the hands of accomplished writers, artists, and composers. Very often an interesting skin ridge pattern (such as a whorl, loop, or composite loop) can be found on this mount, and is said to enhance both instinct and the creative imagination. When small lines move upwards from the base of Luna, intuition and psychic perception are increased (Figure 12.4).

Venus

The mount of Venus reflects our passion and capacity to

Figure 12.3: Lines branching off th
Luna

Figure 12.4: I
nally up the r

love. While some people with a
laughingly reply "sex therapi
favorite career, few actual care
this mount alone.

Nevertheless, a strong mo
sympathy, and passion to th

qualities of
of the other

Unlike a s
prominent m

and commitment. It will make the physician more caring, the teacher more concerned, and the executive more likely to respond to human needs and priorities than to business advantages alone. Many politicians are likely to have a large mount of Venus as well.

The Lines

Saturn: Line of Life Task

Although the mounts and fingers are important guides to career direction, the line of Saturn (also known as the fate line and the career line) reveals how satisfied we are in our career and the degree to which we are fulfilling our life task.

As mentioned earlier, the line of Saturn normally begins at the base of the palm between the mounts of Venus and Luna and moves upwards towards the Saturn finger (Figure 12.5). This would indicate that the individual knew her life path since she was a teenager and began to pursue her career at that time.

Generally speaking, the later the Saturn line begins on the hand, the later in life people will find their true vocation.

- The stronger and clearer the line of Saturn, the more content we are with the direction of our life.

- When the Saturn line runs together with the life line at its commencement (Figure 12.6), it is often diffi-

Figure 12.5: Strong line of Saturn

cult to establish oneself in a career. This may be primarily due to pressure or expectation from parents. When the fate line begins inside the life line, the influence from parents is especially strong.

Figure 12.6: Saturn line running together with the life line at its beginning

- When the line begins in the mount of Luna (Figure 12.7), the person's life path will be extremely varied, with the potential for several careers and frequent relocations. Some palmists believe that a fate line beginning in the Luna mount reveals work in the public eye, which can include anything from a rock star to a teacher or beautician.

Figure 12.7: Saturn line commencing in the mount of Luna

- A fate line that stops at the head line is often found on people who tend to lose their sense of direction or purpose by their late 30's or early 40's (a period often referred to as "mid-life crisis"). They are inclined to "drift" professionally during the latter half of their life, or will tend to be dissatisfied with their chosen line of work.

- Most Saturn lines end at or just above the heart line, indicating a traditional period of employment and subsequent retirement.

- When the Saturn line continues deep into the mount of Saturn, the person will probably remain active well beyond retirement age, and may well continue the present career or develop a new one.

- When the career line ends deep in the mount of Jupiter (Figure 12.8), the career involves leadership.

- When it ends between the mounts of Saturn and Apollo, the career may be related to some aspect of the arts. It can also be an indication of money or fame.

- If the career line is strong and deep, the person will realize the potential the line offers. A strong line also reveals self-confidence, determination, and satisfaction in work.

Figure 12.8: Saturn line ending in Jupiter mount

- Two or more Saturn lines (Figure 12.9) are found in the hands of those who pursue two or more careers (or one career and an important avocation).

- When there is an abundance of weak

Figure 12.9: Several Saturn lines on hand

263

parallel lines—such as four or five—there may be a tendency to scatter one's energy in too many directions.

- The *Ladder of Success* consists of several lines parallel to the fate line near its upper end (Figure 12.10). It indicates a self-made man or woman who has made it to the top through perseverance.

- If the fate line is thin, shallow, or absent (Figure 12.11), there is often a struggle to fulfill one's career ambitions (if indeed these ambitions are defined at all). Frustration and lack of focus are common.

- A small parallel line next to a broken fate line helps

Figure 12.10: The Ladder of Success

Figure 12.11: Weak, shallow Saturn line

strengthen the line, and tends to minimize the challenge or difficulty the broken line represents.

- Islands on the Saturn line reveal a need for a greater focus of both energy and ideas relating to the career. Obstacles to the career are common.

- Breaks on this line (Figure 12.12) reveal periods of transition and possible lack of career direction.

- A wavy Saturn line is a sign of irregular endurance in one's chosen career or direction. Such a person tends to be a "Jack-of-all-trades," as opposed to a specialist in one or two fields.

- Branches moving upwards from this line add strength to the line at the age they appear, while downward branches indicate career disappointments.

- When the Saturn line is absent altogether, the individual will tend to lack stability and professional focus. If found on a good hand—with clear lines, well-shaped fingers and clear skin ridge patterns—the person may take on numerous jobs for short periods of time,

Figure 12.12: Breaks on the Saturn line

265

or jobs with frequent relocations. This commonly results in a life that is both unconventional and adventurous.

- When a Saturn line is missing from a poor hand— one that has misshapen fingers, broken lines, or poor skin ridge formations—it almost always indicates a drifter, a drop-out, or possibly a criminal who has no roots and little chance of success.

The Apollo Line

The presence of a good line of Apollo or Sun line (Figure 12.13a) tends to strengthen the Saturn line. It is found on the hands of many wealthy and successful people, and is also associated with accomplishment in music, entertainment, and the arts. It reveals an ability to land on one's feet in the face of life's challenges as they relate to career. The presence of a good Apollo line is also believed to be an advantage after retirement age, bestowing an ability to adapt to the new demands and opportunities of retirement. Seniors without strong Apollo lines often have difficulty getting on without the structure of regular employment.

Long Apollo lines are rare. They most often consist of a small dash that runs from above the heart line to the base of the Apollo finger.

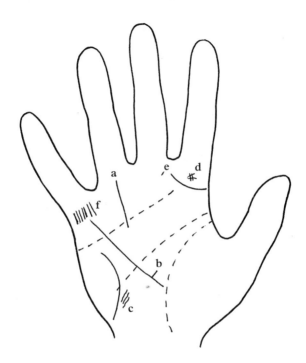

Figure 12.13: Minor lines concerning career

a-Apollo Line
b-Health Line
   (*Mercury line*)
c-Intuition Lines

d-The Teacher's
   Square
e-The Ring of
   Solomon

f-The Medical
   Stigmata

The Health Line (Mercury Line)

While of no direct impact on career, this line (Figure 12.13b) relates to our physical health and particularly that of the stomach and intestinal area.

When the line is fragmented or weak, it indicates a potential for problems in this area of the body, and is found on the hands of people subject to ulcers, colitis, chronic constipation, parasites, and other forms of intestinal problems.

If you're in a high-pressure job, be especially aware of the presence of this line in your hands, and work to minimize stress—or learn how to deal with it—as well as you can.

Intuition Lines

Small diagonal lines that run up the mount of Luna (Figure 12.14) indicate intuition or a degree of psychic ability. When a line is long and continues up towards the mount of Mercury (Figure 12.13c) these abilities are strengthened. Though rare, they are occasionally seen on the hands of clairvoyants and very gifted psychics.

Figure 12.14: Small diagonal lines on Luna

The Teacher's Square

A small square on the mount of Jupiter (Figure 12.13d) indicates a talent for teaching, lecturing, or providing any type of instruction.

People with this special marking may be secondary school teachers or university professors, or do private tutoring, present workshops or seminars, or provide practical instruction in subjects like swimming, yoga, or crafts.

The Ring of Solomon

The Ring of Solomon (Figure 12.13e) consists of a diagonal line (often in the form of an arc) passing through the Jupiter mount.

Traditionally, this line has been linked to a strong interest in metaphysics and proficiency in occult sciences like divination or astrology. However, this line means that one is curious about "what makes people tick," and reveals psychological insight into other people's lives, their hopes, and their dreams.

Often found on good palmists, astrologers, and psychic counselors, it also appears in the hands of capable lawyers, teachers, therapists, and writers. The clearer, deeper, and better-formed the line, the greater and more developed the talent.

The Medical Stigmata

The medical stigmata or "samaritan lines" are made up of a series of tiny vertical lines on the mount of Mercury (Figure 12.13f). People with this pattern like to help others and are often attracted to healing, in professions like physician, nurse, chiropractor, massage therapist, psychologist, or homeopath. Yet those who are attracted to these careers primarily for financial reasons may not have these lines: the medical stigmata appears primarily in the hands of people who are sincerely interested in assisting in the healing of others for its own sake.

★ ★ ★ ★ ★

When we look at the hand in relation to career and life task, we must remember that *no one is a victim of the universe* and that we create our own reality.

13

METAPHYSICAL HANDS

Living a spiritual life does not necessarily involve escaping from the world, nor does it call for the repression of our lower nature; it is grounded in the conscious awareness of who we are as human beings. It also involves integrating our physical body, thoughts, and emotions with our spiritual center, known variously as the Christ Within, the higher self, or the Core.

Some old-fashioned religious doctrines preach that two primary ingredients of spirituality are asceticism and denial. More contemporary goals of spirituality include the establishment of right human relations, the promotion of goodwill, and doing our part towards establishing peace on

Earth. In addition to this outer work, spirituality also implies deepening our connection with our higher self, with Mother Earth, and with the universal consciousness many people call God. While not an easy goal in this workaday world, striving to live a spiritual life today can be a great adventure, full of discovery and enjoyment.

Over the years, serious students of palmistry have used hand analysis to help guide us towards developing our spiritual potential. Nevertheless, several myths persist regarding what constitutes a "spiritual" hand. In most books, long, tapered fingers are seen as a good indication of spiritual potential, along with the presence of mystic crosses, lines of intuition, Rings of Solomon, and other signs. In some cases, these markings have become a status symbol among students of occultism ("Hey, take a look at my mystic cross!"). Also, some hand readers stress the importance of increasing psychic ability over developing intuition and spiritual consciousness through meditation, opening the heart, and selfless service.

The hand is the mirror of our spiritual essence as expressed through our personality, talents, and mental ability, we will see how—by studying basic hand types and markings—we can expand our awareness, develop our intuition, and come into deeper contact with our spiritual core. By integrating these aspects into daily life, we can discover new avenues of spiritual unfoldment and service, according to our energies, talents, and aspirations.

All Hands Are Spiritual Hands

All types of hands—elementary, square, spatulate, conic, and psychic—express essential qualities that enable us to reach spiritual unfoldment and the expansion of consciousness. While these qualities are important by themselves, the hand may also indicate what we need to achieve a deeper level of personal integration and harmony. In many cases, especially where there is dissatisfaction and frustration in life, the existence of a particular quality in the hand may indicate the need to develop a *complementary* quality in order to fully integrate our personality. For example, those who are primarily intellectual might strive to develop their emotional nature, while the person who is primarily sensual might need to develop self-discipline.

While the following brief descriptions of hand types are valuable in evaluating spiritual potential and expression, remember to pay attention to the important modifying factors that appear in the hands, such as lines, mounts, finger spacing, skin ridge patterns, skin texture, and flexibility.

Elementary Hands

We mentioned that people with elementary hands are often very grounded in three-dimensional reality, and function well in the material world. These people are often physically strong, as well as reliable, stable, and practical. They think before they act and prefer to see things in a simple, uncomplicated way. They are naturally attracted to the outdoors, and often work in agriculture, forestry, and the building trades. Many like to work with animals.

From a spiritual point of view, the "earthy" quality of these individuals helps keep them grounded, which means that they are in touch with reality and the ground they stand on. These people are often very much in tune with their physical instincts as well. Many can experience being in tune with Earth energy, and have a special affinity for trees, animals, and other features of the natural world.

- People with elementary hands are often suspicious of spiritual teachings unless they have practical value. To quote the American Indian medicine man Sun Bear: "I don't care what your philosophy is unless it can grow corn."

- People with elementary hands tend to lack pretense and want to see how an idea can work on an everyday level.

- Owners of elementary hands tend to see life in the simplest of terms, without considering other points of view. They can easily become closed-minded and prejudiced as a result.

- They can also be overly cautious and not want to take risks, especially if they have rigid hands. This can keep them stuck in old patterns that need to be relinquished.

From a spiritual point of view, people with elementary hands need to expand their range of interests. Beginning a new hobby, taking adult education classes, traveling, reading, and other activities are useful in helping them appreciate new ideas and other approaches to life.

They are often good healers and have a tremendous capacity for sharing. The opportunity for service as a practical manifestation of spirituality is great.

Spatulate Hands

Those with spatulate hands are high-energy people. They are enthusiastic, emotional, and excitable. They are not resistant to new ideas, nor are they afraid of moving forward into unfamiliar areas of activity and study. They are risk takers. These characteristics are often found in leaders of religious groups and organizers of spiritual events. In spiritual matters—as with all areas of life—there is an innate enthusiasm for discovering, learning, overcoming obstacles, and moving ahead.

- Spatulate fingers tend to be short when compared to the length of the palm itself. This means that their owners tend to see issues on a large scale.

- Unless the fingers are knotted, the owners of spatulate hands don't like to pay attention to details and may scorn careful study and analysis.

- Receptivity may also need to be developed, along with the ability to sit quietly and "go inside."

- If the first phalange of the thumb is thin, there may be a need to reduce stress through exercise, diet, meditation, or through martial arts like tai chi or karate.

- A primary spiritual goal would be to increase receptivity while acknowledging the dynamic, outgoing qualities that these hands represent.

Squarish Hands

The squarish hand reflects primarily an intellectual character. Common sense, order, method, and determination are several of its essential qualities. Administrators, researchers, and teachers often reflect the qualities shown by square hands. They love order, rules, and stability, and can express their ideas in a clear, well-organized manner. While the spatulate hand may express the principle of "spirituality in action," the squarish hand might reflect the principle of "divine order and authority."

Several challenges face people with squarish hands:

- There is often a tendency to be afraid of change and

closed to new ideas, especially if the hand is rigid.

- While healthy skepticism is often useful when deal-ing with metaphysical matters, people with squarish fingertips (especially if the nails are naturally short) are often quite suspicious, demanding that an idea be proven rationally beyond any shadow of a doubt before they will accept it.

- In cases where the hand and thumb are rigid, the sharing—be it feelings, ideas, or possessions—is an important spiritual lesson.

- People with squarish hands need to develop the sen-sual and emotional aspects of the personality, espe-cially if the fingers are thin and knotted.

- People with squarish hands often need to be more spontaneous and learn how to "let go."

- The square-handed individual might consider yoga (to develop flexibility), active sports (to mobilize physical energy), and aerobic dancing to help get "out of the head" and more in tune with body rhythms.

Conic Hands

People with conic hands have little trouble getting in touch with their feelings. They are governed by their emotions and are often drawn to things spiritual. Their conic fingers reveal a keen appreciation of nature, which, with a pointed Jupiter finger (especially if it is long and accompanied by a well-developed mount), reflects a strong inspirational and devotional current.

- Meditation, prayer, chanting, and drugs are often used by conic-handed people to achieve their spiritual ideal.

- They are often drawn to psychic development, especially if there is a pronounced mount of Luna with strong lines of intuition.

- They have the ability to express spiritual ideals through beauty and art, and an innate ability to support others in their spiritual endeavors.

However, people with conic hands have their own unique challenges:

- Conic-handed individuals (especially if the thumb and hand are flexible) have difficulty being consistent. They have a tendency to move quickly from one spiritual group or teaching to another, without developing a sense of depth or commitment.

- They can also be capricious and easily swayed by moods.

- If the hands are thick and soft, there can be an inordinate love for material things and the tendency to focus on the sensual aspects of life at the expense of spirituality.

People with conic fingers can do several things to reach spiritual and psychological integration:

- Generally speaking, the owners of conic hands need to develop the intellect—to analyze and question more, and not be swayed by sentiment and impulse.

- When the fingers are smooth, there is a need to focus more on details.

- The development of order, tact, responsibility, and consistency are also major keys to their spiritual integration.

- If the fingers are knotted, the intellectual tendencies are already an important part of the personality.

- In cases where the hands are thin and crossed by many lines, it may be appropriate to suggest a diet containing whole grains and pulses, with a minimum of sugar, red meat, harsh spices and other stimulants, in order to reduce nervous tension and help stabilize the emotions. Yoga and meditation are good complements to such a diet.

- Finally, spirituality through *service* on a practical level is an important spiritual path for those with conic hands.

Psychic Hands

Although psychic hands are extremely rare in their pure form, they reveal a natural affinity for spirituality and religion. This type of hand reflects all the positive aspects of the conic hand, where love of beauty, harmony, and religious inspiration are pronounced. Meditation, prayer, and philosophy (especially when the fingers are knotted) are favored with this type of hand.

- There is a need to be more grounded in the details of daily living (or at least to have someone else taking care of the "nuts and bolts").

- Because people with psychic hands are highly sensitive, they require pure food and a minimum of alcohol, tobacco, caffeine, and other toxins. Drug abuse can also be a problem.

Because people with psychic hands tend to get lost in dreams and separate from day-to-day reality, it is useful for them to keep in touch with the Earth through activities such as gardening and taking long walks in the country.

- Exercise is also important, especially those forms that strengthen the legs and ankles.

- The need for strong and stable friendships is essential for these people, especially with friends who provide a "grounding" influence.

Philosophical Hands

Hands with knotty joints form a special classification for this chapter, and characterize the religious thinker and scholar. Like the owner of the squarish hand, people with knotty fingers are logical, reasonable, and studious. Such hands are often found in India among yogis, ascetics, and philosophers.

- People with these hands are not seduced by appearances, and have the ability to penetrate deeply into the nature of truth and reality.

- Being inherently patient, they are careful and thorough in their undertakings. As teachers and writers, they can examine all sides of a question and analyze concepts often passed over by others, especially if the fingers are long and one or more composite fingerprints are present.

Philosophical hands also offer unique challenges:

- Individuals with philosophical hands can often get stuck in details and fail to perceive the totality of an issue, especially if the fingers are both knotted and long.

- There may be a tendency to lose oneself in metaphysical concepts without being grounded in everyday reality. A classic example would be a scholar well versed in Hermetic philosophy, but who forgets to eat her dinner and habitually loses her keys.

- Sometimes the analytical understanding of spiritual matters is developed at the expense of following one's gut feelings. As part of the process of spiritual integration, qualities like playfulness, emotionality, and body awareness might be considered.

Mixed Hands

The mixed hand is by far the most common, and by definition reflects many of the traits discussed in the preceding pages. These hands reveal a complexity of currents, talents, and abilities, including an ease in adapting to new situations and an openness to unfamiliar teachings and spiritual practices. Such hands reveal a strong mystical tendency (especially if the Jupiter finger is long and tapered and a mystic cross or Ring of Solomon is present), and an ability to express spiritual understanding in practical terms.

By developing an analytical technique based on sensitivity and careful attention to detail, we can gradually perceive people's inner qualities and offer insights that can help them connect with their Higher Self and achieve their deepest spiritual potential.

The Lines

Particular lines on the hand can offer additional insights into spiritual direction and unfoldment.

The heart line, as mentioned before, indicates the depth and quality of the emotions. In a spiritual context, these emotions—when properly channeled—are essential in helping us attain our spiritual goals.

- Generally speaking, a long, deep, straight, or otherwise predominating heart line (Figure 13.1) reveals a person who is oriented towards universal brotherhood and service to humanity. Contact with other people is favored, whether as a spiritual teacher, healer, administrator, or volunteer in a hospital.

- Shorter or more "physical" heart lines (Figure 13.2) can indicate devotion on a more personal scale, such as towards a particular religious figure or group.

The *head line* is a good indicator of your spiritual direction.

Figure 13.1: Long, deep heart line

Figure 13.2: Shorter, more "physical" heart line

- When the head line predominates over the heart line—being deeper and stronger, as seen in Figure 13.3—the individual will be drawn more towards study, thinking, and meditation than devotional practices like prayer and chanting.

- If the head line moves straight across the palm (Figure 13.4), it indicates a realistic and practical approach towards spirituality.

- A prominent downward slope of the head line (Figure 13.5) reveals that dreams, visions, and instinct play an important role in one's spiritual life. The positive aspects of such a line include an ability

Figure 13.3: Strong head line

Figure 13.4: Straight head line

to grasp abstract or esoteric subjects easily, while the negative aspects include disorganization and difficulty translating spiritual understanding into daily practice. If the head line is islanded as well, there can be a tendency towards poor concentration and an inability to focus.

- Slightly sloping head lines (Figure 13.6) reveal a balance between the realistic and imaginative aspects of spirituality.

Lines of intuition begin in the mount of Luna and move towards the center of the palm (Figure 13.7). They indicate

Figure 13.5: Head line sloping strongly towards mount of Luna

Figure 13.6: Head line with gradual slope towards Luna

strong intuitive ability and the tendency to follow one's instincts rather than rely on analysis.

When a single line of intuition moves from the mount of Luna and forms a gentle arc towards the mount of Mercury (Figure 13.8), strong psychic ability may be present. Known as the *Line of Uranus*, this is sometimes found in the hands of mediums and clairvoyants. It may be accompanied by one or more interesting series of skin ridge patterns on the mount of Luna, which can accentuate the instinctual nature.

The *Ring of Solomon* or *Seal of Solomon* (Figure 13.9) is also found on the hands of many psychic people. It consists of a diagonal line (often in the form of an arc) that passes through the mount of Jupiter. It may also be formed by two

Figure 13.7: Lines of intuition

Figure 13.8: Line of Uranus

parallel lines. This marking shows a strong interest in metaphysics, occultism, and unorthodox religion. It also is found on people who are fascinated by human nature and called upon by others to offer advice and counsel. People with this line are often drawn to careers as psychologists, and take up study in such areas as astrology, palmistry, yoga, and mysticism.

Figure 13.9: Ring of Solomon

The *Mystic Cross* is considered a sign of strong interest in spiritual development. Appearing as a cross between the lines of heart and head, it is not the result of two long lines (such as the Saturn line and an influence line from the mount of Venus) but rather is formed by two short lines that cross each other (Figure 13.10).

Figure 13.10: The Mystic Cross

The absence of these "spiritual" markings does not indicate any lack of spiritual development or capacity, nor should their existence be interpreted as a sign of special spiritual advancement. Rather, these marking—whether alone or collectively—are merely signposts that indicate certain interests and abilities.

Hand analysis provides a master key to help us achieve self-awareness and understand our place in the universe. It teaches that each individual temperament is a unique, equal, and valid reflection of spiritual reality and shows how it can be expressed in a positive and dynamic way from the core of our being. Above all, hand analysis can inspire us to expand our inner vision. To the degree that we are able to release these positive unconscious forces, we are able to help others come upon their innate wisdom, joy, and inner peace.

III

INDIAN
PALMISTRY

Indian palmistry, known as *Samudrika shastra*, can trace its origins back thousands of years. While the so-called Indian school of palmistry (some refer to it as "Hindu palmistry") is somewhat different from both Western palmistry and Chinese palmistry, many modern Indian hand analysts are using Western interpretations in their consultations. Some traditionalists feel that the gradual adoption of Western palmistry with its emphasis on psychology is a betrayal of the ancient roots of Indian palmistry.

In India, palmistry has always been viewed as a sacred science. The human hand is considered a special part of the body that reveals each person's unique *dharma*, or life path for this incarnation. The lines themselves are considered manifestations of God. Early palmistry texts stress that the palmist—the individual who interprets these divine signs on the hand—must adhere to a strict code of personal conduct and not only achieve a deep practical knowledge of palmistry, but a high level of spiritual attainment as well.

Many Indian religions teach that each individual soul experiences many incarnations, and that the circumstances of our present life are determined by our thoughts, words, and deeds from previous lives. By the same token, it is taught that our future lives will be determined by what we do in *this* life: how we take care of our health, how we create and maintain our relationships with others, the type of work we do, and how we unfold and express our innate spiritual nature.

Many Indian spiritual teachers believe that by developing self-knowledge, we can tap into the energy, talents, and interests that we may have brought with us into our present life. As we develop our self-understanding, we create our own future, not only in this life, but in future ones as well.

14

THE PALM AND ITS CHARACTERISTICS

Many of the teachings regarding the size, shape, thickness, and consistency of the palm are similar in Indian and Western palmistry.

The well-known Hindu palmist K.C. Sen listed the ten signs of a "good" hand in his book *Hast Samudrika Shastra*. Some reflect the different racial types who live in India today.

1. The hands are warm to the touch.

2. The skin color of the upturned palm is "like the sky before the dawn," or a deep pink.

3. When the hand is opened, the fingers are held close together without any openings between them.

4. The skin texture of the hands is shiny "as if they are oiled."

5. The consistency of the hand is full and thick, yet without being flabby or soft.

6. The hands are neither too large nor too small in relation to the person's body size.

7. The nails are copper-colored.

8. The fingers are long. (As in Chinese palmistry, if the length of the middle finger is greater than the length of the palm, the fingers are considered long.)

9. The palms are broad rather than long and thin.

10. Under normal circumstances, the hands are dry to the touch, as opposed to damp and sweaty.

According to traditional Hindu palmists, other specific characteristics of the palm have individual meanings:

- Hard hands: strong willed; tenacious; good in business; likes to get up early in the morning

- Soft hands: lethargic yet restless; loves luxury and comfort

- Well-formed hands and long fingers (on men): wealth

- Skinny hands with protruding veins on back of hands (on women): unhappiness

- Raised mounts on thick palms: charitable character
- Marked hollowness in the center of the palm: person will lose inheritance from parents; poverty
- Palm with thick, heavy lines: difficulties in life
- Palm with very few lines: poverty

Hand Types

Many of the classifications of hands are identical to the hand types discussed earlier. However, Indian palmists have sometimes offered different interpretations.

Rudimentary Hands

Rudimentary hands are similar to the elementary hands described earlier, and are found on simple, straightforward people. In India, people with these hands would likely be involved in the most menial types of jobs.

Square Hands

Indian palmists have depicted people with square hands as having a quiet temperament and an inquiring disposition; however, some believe that people with squarish hands are prone to mischief and can cause public scandal.

Spatulate Hands

In India, people with spatulate hands seem to encompass a wide range of behavior. On one hand, they are hard-working people who like to be on time. However, spatulate hands are also found on pleasure-seekers.

Conic Hands

Conic hands are not highly valued in India. Several authors have stated that people with conic hands are basically selfish and hungry for fame and recognition. In addition, conic hands indicate a sensuous nature.

Philosophical Hands

People with philosophical hands are depicted as deep thinkers who are seekers of truth. People with these hands (which appear to be more common in India than in Europe or North America) enjoy studying psychology, philosophy, and metaphysics.

Mixed Hands

Mixed hands reveal a person who can excel in several specialized areas of work or study.

Color of the Palm

Hindu palmists pay close attention to the color of the skin, especially on the front of the hand. Taking into account that many Indian people have darker skin than many Americans or Europeans, the colors have the following basic meanings:

- Red or pink color: good health; general good fortune
- Yellowish color: liver problems; may also be a sign of habitual sexual over-indulgence
- Bluish color: Over-indulgence in alcohol or drugs
- Whitish color: low energy; poverty

The Mounts of the Hand

The Kartikeyan system of palmistry, which developed in southern India centuries ago, teaches that there are different regions of the hand (known in Sanskrit as *sthanas*, or "places") on which are engraved lines known as *rekhas*. Although both hands are important in Indian palmistry, hand analysts tend to focus on a man's right hand and a woman's left hand. However, the significance of certain markings may differ according to the hand on which is it found.

As part of the Indian school of palmistry, the Kartikeyan system teaches that there are ten basic regions of the hand and fingers. While most correspond to the mounts found in

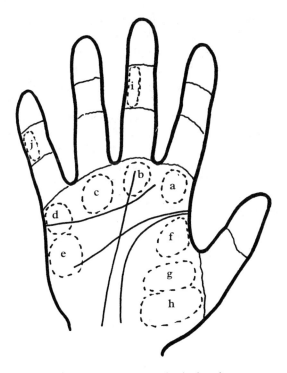

Figure 14.1: The ten sthanas as seen in the hand

a-Pithru sthana   e-Dharma sthana   i- Putra sankhya
b-Mathru sthana   f- Sathru sthana   sthana
c-Vidya sthana   g-Brathru sthana   j-Putra sthana
d-Jaya sthana   h-Bandhu sthana

Western palmistry, their significance is often quite different. In contrast to the mounts of Western palmistry, these sthanas usually do not have great significance in themselves. Rather, they are seen as a *blank canvas* on which distinct palmar markings offer important insights into the person's health, character, and future endeavors. For this reason, most books about Indian palmistry follow the Western system of classifying the mounts according to different planets. More often than not, they also provide interpretations that are similar to books written by Western hand analysts.

Pithru Sthana

The *Pithru sthana* (Figure 14.1a) is located beneath the index (Jupiter) finger.

Mathru Sthana

The *Mathru sthana* (Figure 14.1b), corresponds to the Saturn mount.

Vidya Sthana

The *Vidya sthana* (Figure 14.1c) is the pad located beneath the ring finger, corresponding to the mount of Apollo.

Jaya Sthana

The *Jaya sthana* (Figure 14.1d) is in a location similar to that of the mount of Mercury.

Dharma Sthana

The location of *Dharma sthana* (Figure 14.1e) corresponds to what Westerns call the upper mount of Mars, located below the beginning of the heart line.

Sathru Sthana

The *Sathru sthana* (Figure 14.1f) is found in the depression of the palm, which roughly corresponds to the lower mount of Mars in Western palmistry. The word "sathru" means "foe."

Brathru Sthana

This mount, known in India as *Brathru sthana* (the sthana of brothers), is located in the upper half of the Venus mount (Figure 14.1g).

Bandhu Sthana

The *Bandhu sthana*, or "the place of relatives," is found in the lower part of the mount of Venus (Figure 14.1h).

In addition to the eight major *sthanas* found on the palm, Indian palmistry recognizes two additional sthanas on the middle and little fingers. The left half of the middle phalange of the middle finger is called *Putra Sankhya Sthana* (Figure 14.1i), or "the place of the number of sons," while the left half of the middle phalange of the little finger is called the *Putra Sthana,* or "the place of sons" (Figure 14.1j).

In the following chapters, we will examine some of the dozens of markings found on the *sthanas* and explore their significance.

15

FINGERS AND NAILS

A detailed study of the fingers and nails is very important to Indian palmists. Although many contemporary Indian palmists ascribe the same qualities to the fingers and nails that Western palmists do, books that focus on traditional Indian or Hindu palmistry often offer very different interpretations—some appearing unusual and even extreme to many Western readers. Here we will examine some of the Indian interpretations of various aspects of the fingers and fingernails, taking into account the many different cultural and religious traditions found in this fascinating land.

Long, slender fingers with conic tips (Figure 15.1) have always been highly regarded in India. Many Hindu saints—such as the Lord Krishna—possessed such hands. On a practical everyday level, which involves holding down a job and sticking to a budget, these hands are far from ideal.

They reveal an impractical individual who may have difficulty focusing on the material needs of others. However, for those who already have a source of steady income and wish to develop their artistic, intellectual, or spiritual capacities, such a hand is perfect.

Hindu palmists have offered the following observations regarding specific finger characteristics:

Figure 15.1: Hand with long, slender fingers with conic tips

- Straight fingers: overall good fortune

- Fingers that are straight and long: long life; tendency to hide one's feelings

- Crooked fingers (on males): poverty

- Crooked fingers (on females): childlessness or widowhood

- Fingers that are thick and round: difficulty in handling money; poverty

- Fingers that are short and flat (with flat tips): low economic status; destined for menial jobs

- Dry fingers: low economic status
- Closed fingers (on open hand): wealth; ability to save money
- Gaps between the fingers (when fingers held together): poverty
- Gap between base of index and middle fingers (Figure 15.2): careless; impulsive; unconventional
- Gap between base of middle and ring fingers (Figure 15.3): unconventional personality; may lack discretion

Figure 15.2: Gap between base of index finger and middle finger

Figure 15.3: Gap between base of middle finger and ring finger

- Gap between base of ring and little fingers: head-strong and opinionated
- Fingertips bending back: tenacious nature
- Stiff fingertips that do not bend back: greedy
- Long top phalanges: ability to work skillfully with one's hands (such as carpenters, artists, hairdressers, surgeons, sculptors)
- Thin, weak lower phalanges: shy, retiring personality
- Thick, fleshy lower phalanges: tendency to overindulge in food and drink; greedy
- Long little finger (reaching the top phalange of the ring finger): success through his or her own efforts.
- Extra fingers or partly formed extra fingers: poverty; troubles in relationships; possible short life

The Thumb

Traditional Indian palmists believe that the thumb is the most important finger of the hand. It is said that, in some parts of India, palmists focus their attention on the human thumb alone. Many of the Western interpretations regarding the thumb have been adopted by contemporary Indian palmists. What follows are those observations that differ.

Generally speaking, traditional Indian palmists teach that a thumb should be relatively long and roundish; the upper and lower phalanges should be of similar proportions; and the thumb tip should reach the second phalange of the index finger. People with this type of finger are believed to possess a sound physical constitution and have a strong aptitude for higher education, especially in engineering, design, and the sciences. By contrast, Hindu palmists believe that thumbs that are short, flat, and crooked spell misfortune, whether in marriage, health, or career.

- Low-set thumb: adaptable personality, independent; generous; intelligent
- High-set thumb: lower intelligence; rigid and narrow-minded personality
- Supple thumb: trouble holding onto money
- Firm thumb: stable, reliable personality; strong will
- Stiff thumb: greedy; rigid personality
- Small thumb: guided by emotions; lack of determination
- Large thumb: guided more by the intellect than by the emotions
- Round, strong, slightly flexible thumbs: overall good fortune in health, marriage, and career
- Short thumb with a flat tip: prone to misfortune in all areas of life
- Wide upper phalange (on female hand): widowhood

- Wide upper phalange (on male hand): bachelorhood
- Wide upper phalange and waisted lower phalange: argumentative nature; difficulties in relationships
- Long first phalange: self-reliant, strong willpower
- Short first phalange: propensity for evil; difficulty in establishing and maintaining relationships with members of the opposite sex
- Conic tip: diplomatic nature
- Long and thick second phalange: logical thinker; easily grasps difference between right and wrong
- Short and thin second phalange: poor judgment; deficient intellect
- Thick lower phalange: frequent travel
- Rounded, fleshy thumb (on female hand): will marry into wealth

Other Fingers

Indian palmists generally ascribe the same qualities to individual fingers as Western palmists. However, different interpretations sometimes exist, especially in regard to personality and health.

Index Finger

- Index finger the same length as middle finger: prideful nature; conceited; snobbish
- Crooked top phalange of index finger: potential for lung disease
- Index finger leaning towards middle finger: prideful nature

Middle Finger

- Very long: tendency towards glandular diseases
- Crooked top phalange: violent temper; tendency towards abdominal problems
- Conic top phalange: volatile, excitable character
- Middle finger leaning towards index finger: overly-superstitious nature
- Middle finger leaning towards ring finger: increased optimism and cheerfulness

Ring Finger

- Ring finger the same size as index finger: professional success in arts and music

- Ring finger longer than index finger: strong artistic ability
- Ring finger the same size as middle finger: sign of a gambler
- Crooked top phalange of ring finger: potential for scandal of a sexual nature
- Ring finger leaning towards middle finger: tendency to become sad and depressed

Little Finger

- Little finger whose tip reaches halfway up top phalange of the ring finger: sign of intelligence and excellence as a scholar
- Little finger that is the same length as the ring finger: sign of a genius IQ
- Very short little finger (one whose tip does not reach the base of the top phalange of the ring finger): paranoid tendencies; potential to remain sexually immature as an adult
- Pointed tip on little finger: potential for glandular problems
- Very small and deformed little finger (on female hand): poor ovarian function

- Little finger leaning towards ring finger: creativity in one's career

The Three Parvas

In addition to the "places" on the palm, Indian hand analysts recognize the different phalanges of the fingers, known in Sanskrit as *parvas* (Figure 15.4). Ideally, each parva should be of equal length and of similar proportions. The top phalange is said to represent the mental world. The second or middle phalange represents the material world, while the third or base phalange reflects aspects of the sensual world. The longer the phalange of a particular finger—in comparison to the others—the stronger the qualities that it represents.

- A long, well-developed first phalange on all the fingers is a sign of a person with high aspirations.
- People whose second phalanges are well developed tend to do a lot of thinking and enjoy studying and investigation.

Figure 15.4: The three parvas

- When the bases of the third phalanges are thick and long, the person loves the sensual pleasures of life, such as food, sex, and luxurious surroundings.

Long First or Top Phalange

- On index finger: strong emotions; sensitivity; the ability to be inspired and inspire others; when conic, strong religious devotion
- On middle finger: tendency to want to be alone; if bent towards ring finger: melancholy; if conic, excitable temper
- On ring finger: strong creativity, especially in art and design
- On little finger: good communicator; strong intuition, especially in science, mathematics, and healing

Long Middle or Second Phalange

- On index finger: practical; ability to get things done
- On middle finger: works well on his or her own; good researcher and investigator; enjoys working with plants and machinery; talent for working with medicinal herbs

- On ring finger: ability to work in an artistic field, including interior design, landscape design, or architecture; favors a career in music or theater; proficiency in working with ceramics
- On little finger: ability to work in areas of science, mathematics, and healing; talent for business

Long and Thick Third or Base Phalange

- On index finger: good business sense; enjoys luxury
- On middle finger: tendency to be greedy and acquisitive
- On ring finger: love of being surrounded by beautiful (and often expensive) things
- On little finger—long: shrewd; prone to dishonesty
- On little finger—thick: tendency towards overindulgence in food, alcohol, and sex

Nails

Although long considered a reliable indicator of human character, the nails have also been believed by Indian palmists to be a clear barometer of a person's health.

Ideally, the nails should be slightly longer than they are

wide, with a shiny appearance. People who possess this type of nail are considered pleasant characters—healthy and refined.

- *Long nails* (Figure 15.5): weak physical constitution; tendency for heart and lung diseases, especially when nails are also curved and thin. They also are a sign of an open-minded individual who is tolerant of other points of view.

Figure 15.5: Long nail

- *Long nails with whitish hue:* person of good character who can be relied upon

- *Long, thick, and curved nails:* considered a sign of loose morals; cruel tendencies

- *Narrow and long:* shrewd personality

- *Narrow, long, and curved:* back problems

- *Fan-shaped* (Figure 15.6): back problems; throat diseases

Figure 15.6: Fan-shaped nail

- *Short, thin, and flat:* tendency to be critical and quarrelsome; person is quick to anger; tendency towards heart disease

- *Nails with white spots:* highly strung, nervous personality
- *White spot on thumb nail:* love affair
- *White spot on nail of index finger:* person will profit from a business deal
- *White spot on nail of middle finger:* upcoming voyage by sea
- *White spot on nail of ring finger:* honor and wealth
- *White spot on nail of little finger:* success in business
- *Nails with black spots:* sorrow, grief
- *Black spot on thumb nail:* illicit love affair
- *Black spot on nail of index finger:* loss of wealth due to a bad business deal
- *Black spot on nail of middle finger:* premature death
- *Black spot on nail of ring finger:* scandal
- *Black spot on nail of little finger:* untimely, sudden death
- *Nails with yellowish marks:* impending death
- *Beau's lines—deep furrows running across the nail* (Figure 15.7): a severe illness has adversely affected the nervous system.

Figure 15.7: Beau's lines on nail

16

THE LINES

As in Western palmistry, understanding the significance of the various lines (*rekhas*) is essential to a careful hand analysis. Although some modern Indian palmists have adopted the Western meanings of the major lines, traditional palmists consider these lines to have a different significance.

Hindu palmists have long taught that the left hand contains lines and markings that reflect our actions in past incarnations. In other words, the left hand shows our *inheritance* from previous lifetimes and what we are "born with" in this life. The right hand shows what we are making of the health, talents, and personality traits we have inherited from the past.

The way traditional Indian palmists determine age is unique. According to custom, they measure a line on the hand with a piece of hair from an elephant's tail. When placed across the line, the width of the hair is said to be equivalent to one year of the person's life.

Clear, deep, pinkish, and long lines are considered the best kind to have. They reveal:

- steadiness of purpose
- good health; strong physical constitution
- strength of character; courage

By contrast, weak, shallow, and broken lines have more negative meanings:

- poor health; weak physical constitution
- lack of clearly defined goals in life
- lack of courage
- tendency to scatter one's energies
- loss of wealth (especially when broken)
- loss of memory (especially when the strength of the lines is uneven)

Hindu palmists also believe that the color of the lines have special meanings:

- Pink, clear, narrow lines: wealth

- Pale, whitish lines: poverty
- Reddish lines: strong personality; abundant energy
- Yellowish, golden lines: selfish, inhibited personality
- Brownish lines: spiteful, unforgiving nature

On the following pages, let's examine some of the major lines and their meanings.

Atma Rekha (Rohini)

Atma Rekha, which is also known variously as the "father line," *Gothra rekha, Pitri rekha,* and *Rohini* (Figure 16.1a), corresponds to the life line of Western palmistry. However, instead of beginning above the thumb joint as the life line does, Indian palmists teach that it begins at the base of the hand near the wrist. In some cases, it starts at the *Mani Bandha rekha,* or what Westerners know as the Rascettes of Venus (Figure 16.2). Indian palmists believe, as we do, that the individual is able to increase the length of this line by changes in attitude, as well as lifestyle changes such as diet and exercise.

Like the life line, *Atma rekha* is believed to indicate the potential length of life. Ideally, it should be slightly reddish in color, indicating good health and strong physical constitution. Gaps, breaks, and islands can be signs of serious illness or accident.

ieved to reflect the influences of several of the sthanas
us affect the entire life. Generally speaking, the longer
e, the greater the potential for longevity.

n Rekha (Matri rekha)

Western head line is called *Dhan rekha*, "mother line,"
the Hindus (Figure 16.1c). Like the head line, *Dhan*
a reflects the mental processes, including reasoning
ity, imagination, self-control, and clarity of mind.
Among the early Hindus, it was believed that the length
clarity of this line re-
led one's potential wealth
d material possessions,
cause the careful use of
elligence and reasoning
wers would naturally lead
ower, position, and eco-
ic abundance.

this line is connected
the *Atma rekha* (Figure
), Indian palmists con-
that it is a sign of good
e in that the person is
to accumulate much
ty.

**Figure 16.5: Dhan rekha con-
nected to Atma rekha**

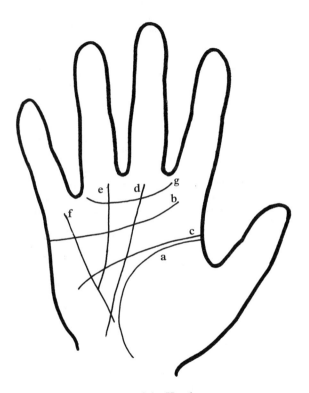

Figure 16.1: The Major Lines of the Hand

a. Atma rekha	d. Indira rekha	g. Mandoshnada
b. Bandha rekha	e. Kamala rekha	rekha
c. Dhan rekha	f . Bala rekha	

Figure 16.2: Atma rekha beginning at Mani Bandha rekha

Figure 16.3: Atma rekha "ending" at base of index finger

If it moves right into the base of the index finger (Figure 16.3), the person is destined to live at least a hundred years.

If this lines contains a branch running up towards the *Pithru sthana* (Figure 16.4), the person will attain a high position in his or her chosen profession.

If a small dot appears on

Figure 16.4: Branch from Atma rekha towards Pithru sthana

this line, it foretells the birth of a son at the a   is b dot appears. However, if the dot is black i   and person will be involved in a scandal.   the

When found on a woman's hand, a small sta at the end of this line indicates widowhood.

Bandha Rekha (Ayu Rekha)

Bandha rekha (Figure 16.1b) corresponds to the hea Western palmistry. While in the West the line is begin at the percussion of the hand under the m Mercury and end near the Jupiter or Saturn finger tional Hindu palmists believe that this line ends und *Jaya sthana* (mount of Mercury).

Although many modern Indian palmists believ characteristics and meanings of this line are simila of the West, traditional Hindu palmists teach that like a life line or a "line of character."

The Sanskrit term *bandha* has to do with the cept of bondage, or life on this earth. When t begins at the base of the index finger, ends a sion of the hand, and is free from breaks or c Hindu palmists believe that the person will li dred years.

Because *Bandha rekha* moves across the to

Indira Rekha

Named for Indira, the Hindu Goddess of Wealth, this line (Figure 16.1d) corresponds to both the Destiny line (in Western palmistry) and the Column of Jade of the Chinese school. The longer, deeper, and clearer the line, the greater the chances of achieving career success and enjoying material abundance throughout life. According to tradition, you need to read this line on the right hand of males and on the left hand of females.

Ideally, this line should begin at the base of the hand (just above the *Mani Bandha rekha*) and be long, clear, and straight, ending at or beyond the joint of the middle finger. Breaks in this line indicate financial reversals and crises in one's professional life. Traditionally, it was believed that a broken *Indira rekha* on the hand of a woman indicated that she would become a widow.

If this line begins within what Westerners call the mount of Luna (Figure 16.6), it means that the career depends on the decisions and caprices of other people rather than our own efforts alone.

If this line begins within the *Atma rekha* or life line (Figure 16.7), the career is dependent on the family's influence, especially its social or economic status. A person who would join the family business, or be hired by a company due to a parent's influence or social position, would likely have such a line in the hand.

Figure 16.6: Indira rekha
beginning on Mount of Luna

Figure 16.7: Indira rekha
beginning within Atma rekha

Kamala Rekha and *Vidya Rekha*

Often accompanying a strong *Indira rekha*, the *Kamala rekha* (Figure 16.1e) corresponds to the Apollo line. When it is long, clear, and strong, it indicates long life, wealth, and renown.

If this line moves from the base of the hand well into the second phalange of the ring finger (Figure 16.8), it is called *Vidya rekha,* or the "line of learning." A highly favorable line, its presence indicates that the person will achieve a high degree of knowledge in the arts and sciences, and fame as an author, professor, or scientist. Like the *Kamala rekha,* it also foretells wealth and longevity.

Figure 16.8: Vidya rekha

Bala Rekha

The location of *Bala rekha* (Figure 16.1f) corresponds to the Mercury or stomach line. When clear, long, free of breaks, and slightly golden in color, it is a sign that the person will enjoy long life and maintain a youthful appearance even in old age.

Mandoshnada Rekha

The meaning of this line (Figure 16.1g), which can be equated to the Girdle of Venus, is a subject of controversy among Indian palmists. Students of the Kartikeyan system believe that this line reveals a cold heart and a dull intellect, with its owner having poor career possibilities in life. Other palmists claim that when this line is clear, well formed, and pinkish in color, it reveals a person with high literary tastes and strong abilities as a writer. However, if the line is broken, poorly formed, and pale in color, the person is greedy and selfish.

If the line tends to be short and runs from the base of the middle finger to the base of the little finger (Figure 16.9), the person will likely be a liar and a cheat.

Figure 16.9: Mandoshnada rekha (short)

Mani-Bandha Rekha

While similar in appearance to the Rascettes of Venus, *Mani-Bandha Rekha* (also known as *Yav Mala*) has a variety of meanings.

- One bracelet with several islands (Figure 16.10): a life of poverty

- Two bracelets with several islands each: a reasonably happy life

- Three bracelets with several islands each (Figure 16.11): a life of wealth and happiness

- If two bracelets go completely around the wrist: great wealth and wisdom

- If three bracelets go completely around the wrist: an exalted position in life, with great wealth, power, and influence. However, if lines are badly chained, life will be difficult. Eventual success, however, is assured through intense personal effort.

Figure 16.10: One bracelet
with several islands

Figure 16.11: Three bracelets
with several islands

Pasa Rekha

This formation has no corresponding line in Western palmistry.
Though rarely found in its pure state, it is formed by an oval
that appears in the center of the palm (Figure 16.12). It is a sign
that the person will be able to overcome all of life's obstacles.

Kamahastika Rekha

A small line beginning above the *Bandha rekha* and moving
towards the middle finger (Figure 16.13), the *Kamahastika*

Figure 16.12: Pasa rekha

Figure 16.13: Kamahastika rekha

rekha often runs parallel to the *Indira rekha* or destiny line. Whenever it appears, it is a sign of good fortune. When found on a man's hand, it foretells happiness from one's children; if found on a woman's hand, she will enjoy abundant wealth and overall good fortune.

Korpara Rekha

Considered important if found only on the left hand, this sign consists of three, four, or five parallel vertical lines that form a cluster under the ring finger (Figure 16.14). Their presence indicates frequent travel.

Figure 16.14: Korpara rekha   Figure 16.15: Dharani rekha

Dharani Rekha

Consisting of a vertical line rising just above the joint at the base of the index finger (Figure 16.15), *Dharani* favors the accumulation of large real estate holdings.

Hemavalli Rekha

The presence of this small line reaching to the ring finger (Figure 16.16) is considered quite favorable by teachers of Kartikeyan palmistry, because it is a sign that the person will enjoy sexual pleasure from youth through old age.

Varistha Rekha

Consisting of several strong vertical lines on the phalange of the index finger (Figure 16.17), *Varistha rekha* has to do with one's extended family. It not only indicates that the person has many aunts, uncles, or cousins, but that relatives will help the person attain his or her goals in life.

Diksha Rekha

Similar in form to the Ring of Solomon, this small line moves diagonally across the *Pithru sthana* (Figure 16.18). Known as the "line of renunciation," it is found on the hands of people who lead a life of sacrifice and service to others.

Figure 16.16: Hemavalli rekha

Figure 16.17: Varistha rekha

Hara rekha

This line forms a small ring around the middle finger (Figure 16.19). Traditionally, the presence of *hara* was a sign of good fortune, due to its purported connection to royalty. If found on a man's hand, it would make him "beloved by his king"; today, this could mean that he would be a protégé of a high-ranking public official, popular entertainer, or company president.

If *hara* appeared on a woman's hand, it indicated that she would be favored as a royal consort or concubine. Like contemporary males, such women today would more likely become associated with important leaders in entertainment, business, or politics, and not necessarily as a sexual partner.

Figure 16.18: Diksha rekha

Figure 16.19: Hara rekha

Triangle of Mars

This triangle is formed by the *Atma rekha*, *Dhan rekha*, and *Bala rekha* (Figure 16.20). When it is well marked, distinct, and unbroken, it is considered a sign of a prosperous, healthy, and long life.

However, if the angles formed by these lines are unusually wide or unusually narrow, some specific interpretations may apply:

- If "a" is wide: sign of a tenderhearted person
- If "a" is narrow: person tends to be foolish and impolitic
- If "b" is wide: long life; good memory; person is mischievous and easily excited
- If "b" is narrow: person is restless and unsettled in life
- If "c" is wide: healthy; honest
- If "c" is narrow: greedy; weak intellect

The Quadrangle

The Quadrangle is formed by the *Dhan rekha*, *Bandha rekha*, *Indira rekha*, and *Bala rekha* (Figure 16.21). Like the Triangle of Mars, the appearance of the Quadrangle has different interpretations in Indian palmistry:

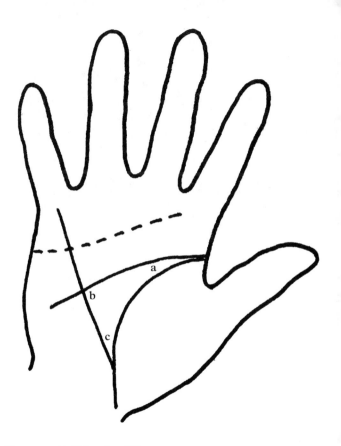

Figure 16.20: Triangle of Mars

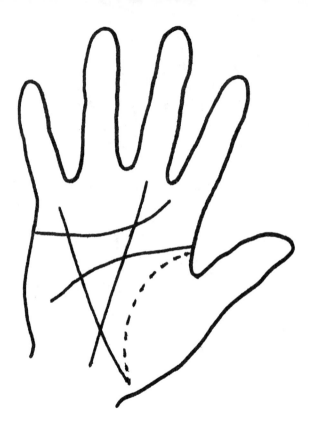

Figure 16.21: The Quadrangle

- If broad and squarish: person is highly principled and loyal
- If the space between *Dhan rekha* and *Bandha rekha* is wide: person tends to be trustworthy
- If the space between *Dhan rekha* and *Bandha rekha* is narrow: person tends to be malicious, greedy, and deceitful
- If the space closest to *Dharma rekha* is narrower than the space under *Vidya sthana:* person tends to be greedy and closed-minded
- If the *Indira rekha* and the *Bala rekha* are indistinct: person tends to be secretive and greedy

Mahi Rekha

Mahi rekha (Figure 16.22) consists of a clear and unbroken line (one that is not crossed or broken by other lines), moving slightly downwards from the edge of the *Jaya sthana*, or mount of Mercury. Long considered a favorable sign, it reveals that its owner is destined to learn the meaning of all the *Shastras*, or the Hindu texts of Divine Law. If found in the hand of a non-Hindu, it would conceivably mean that he or she would become a noted Bible scholar, a teacher of the Kabbalah, or an authority on the Holy Koran.

Figure 16.22: Mahi rekha   Figure 16.23: Jaya rekha

Jaya Rekha

Also known as *hridgata-hatwada*, these small lines (Figure 16.23) are similar to the union lines of Western palmistry, and represent marriage partners. Branches at the end of a line indicate separation. If a line droops towards the *Bandha rekha* (Figure 16.24), it is a sign that the person's partner will die before him or her.

Lines Depicting Brothers and Sisters

A number of lines, known as *Kanishthra rekha*, are similar in form to influence lines. Beginning below the thumb and

Figure 16.24: Jaya rekha drooping towards Bandha rekha

Figure 16.25: Lines indicating siblings

moving across the end of what the Hindus call *Atma rekha* and towards the index finger (Figure 16.25), each line indicates a brother or sister; the deeper ones are brothers and the thinner lines are sisters.

Other palmists teach that small horizontal lines, located at the percussion of the right hand in an area of the upper mount of Mars

Figure 16.26: Lines indicating brothers

(Figure 16.26), indicate the number of brothers one has (or is likely to have). Sister lines are located along the percussion of the right hand in the region of the Lunar mount (Figure 16.27).

Lines Indicating Children

Figure 16.27: Lines indicating sisters

Children have always been thought important in India, and although family planning has begun to limit their size, Indians traditionally have large families. In a country where extended families are the most important social unit, couples who do not have children are considered a disgrace. For these reasons, it is not surprising that there are several methods for reading children in a person's hand.

In Hindu palmistry, it is believed that small lines on the *Satru sthana*, running parallel to the *Atma rekha* or life line, indicate the number of children one will have (Figure 16.28).

When clear vertical lines are found on the *Putrasankhya* sthana or the *Putra sthana* (Figure 16.29), it is believed to

Figure 16.28: Lines indicating children

Figure 16.29: Lines indicating prominent children

indicate the number of prominent children one will have.

Children lines can also be seen at the base of the palm, running parallel to the lower joint of the thumb. A thick and long line is supposed to indicate a son, while a thin and short line reveals a daughter. Figure 16.30 shows that the person will have three daughters and one son. If the line is very short and weak, the child will likely be sickly or die at an early age.

Islands found in the lower thumb joint of the right hand (Figure 16.31) are believed to indicate children as well: each island represents a son or daughter.

Other Lines on the Fingers

Indian palmists take great care in examining any small or thin lines that appear on the fingers. While they may not be the most important lines on the hand, they are believed to reveal important trends in a person's life and can substantially alter the significance of other lines and markings. Some lines on the fingers have already been discussed. Here are others that are important:

Figure 16.30: Lines indicating three daughters and one son

Index finger

- A line beginning at the base of the finger and ending in the second phalange (Figure 16.32): a thoughtful and wise person; strong sense of pride

Figure 16.31: Lines indicating children

340

- Horizontal lines across top phalange: inheritance

- Small vertical lines on second phalange (Figure 16.33): many children

- Small vertical lines on third phalange: jovial disposition

Figure 16.32: Line ending in second phalange of index finger

Figure 16.33: Small vertical lines in second phalange

Figure 16.34: Vertical lines traversing middle finger

Middle Finger

- Several vertical lines traversing the entire middle finger (Figure 16.34): success in mining
- Several vertical lines on top phalange (Figure 16.35): greedy
- Several vertical lines on the third phalange (Figure 16.36): misfortune

Ring Finger

- One straight vertical line from the third to the first

Figure 16.35: Vertical lines on top phalange of middle finger

Figure 16.36: Small vertical lines on third phalange of middle finger

phalange (Figure 16.37): great good fortune

- Two or more straight vertical lines from the third to the first phalange: will lose money due to illicit romantic affairs

- One straight vertical line from the third phalange to the second phalange: person is extravagant with money

Figure 16.37: One straight line from third to first phalange of ring finger

- Several small vertical lines on middle phalange: fame.

Little Finger

- One straight line from the third to the first phalange: mark of strong spirituality; sign of a deep thinker and scholar, especially in philosophy or religion

- Deep line on first phalange (Figure 16.38): delicate health

- Two or more straight vertical lines on the second

Figure 16.38: Deep line on little finger

Figure 16.39: Two lines on second phalange of little finger

phalange (Figure 16.39): good in occult sciences (astrology, palmistry, tarot, esoteric healing)

- Cross bars on second phalange (Figure 16.40): sign of a thief or deceitful person
- Line from *Jaya sthana* to second phalange of little finger (Figure 16.41): sign of a "self-made" man or woman

The Thumb

- Four horizontal lines on second phalange (Figure 16.42): fame and wealth

Figure 16.40: Cross bars on second phalange of little finger

Figure 16.41: Line from Jaya sthana into second phalange of little finger

Figure 16.42: Four horizontal lines on lower phalange of thumb

Figure 16.43: Lines from Brathru sthana into top phalange of thumb

- Two or more lines from *Brathru sthana* into first phalange (Figure 16.43): the person is ardent and sincere in love
- Two or more lines from *Brathru sthana* into the second phalange: person is the object of universal affection among friends, family, and acquaintances.

17

SIGNS AND
SYMBOLS

Indian palmistry teaches that specialized signs and symbols are found throughout the palm and fingers. Some of them have specific meanings, while others reveal a general quality, such as "good fortune" or "happy marriage." Several signs are extremely rare and are found only on the hands of saints and other extraordinary individuals. Since there are literally hundreds of specialized markings, we will cover only some of the most common here.

The Canopy

Considered a rare sign, the Canopy (Figure 17.1) is a symbol of high spiritual and moral attainment wherever it appears on the palm. It is sometimes found on yogis and saints, but can appear on the hands of learned scholars, writers, and teachers as well.

The Circle

In Hindu palmistry, some practitioners believe that a circle is significant only when found on the top phalange (*parva*) of the fingers and thumb. It is believed that these tiny circles (only slightly larger than a dot) tend to cluster in groups of up to ten, and have the following (and sometimes curious) meanings:

Figure 17.1: The Canopy

Figure 17.2: Two tiny circles

- One circle: the person is clever
- Two circles (Figure 17.2): he or she is attractive

- Three circles: the individual is (or will be) wealthy
- Four circles: the person is (or will be) poor
- Five circles (Figure 17.3): he or she is well educated
- Six circles: he or she is intelligent

Figure 17.3: Five tiny circles

- Seven circles: the person will lead a solitary life
- Eight circles: the person is (or will be) poor
- Nine circles: the individual will be distinguished as a government leader
- Ten circles: the person will be employed as a civil servant

Other Indian palmists maintain that the presence of a larger single circle or oval will sometimes have special significance, depending on where it is found on the palm and fingers.

- When found under the ring finger (Figure 17.4): fame and wealth

- When located on the
  mount of Luna:
  danger and death by
  drowning

- When a single circle is
  found anywhere else
  on the hand or fingers:
  misfortune

Figure 17.4: Circle under the ring finger

The Cross

The cross—composed of
two small, distinct lines that
are not part of any other line—is generally considered an
unfavorable sign to have, with two exceptions:

- When located on the *Pithru sthana*: happy marriage

- When found on *Vidya sthana*: person will achieve
  fame and wealth

- When appearing on the *Mathra sthana* and touching
  the *Indira rekha*: sign of possible accident and premature death

- When found on *Jaya sthana*: the person is a liar and
  a thief

- When found on *Dharma sthana*: sign of an obstinate
  and quarrelsome nature

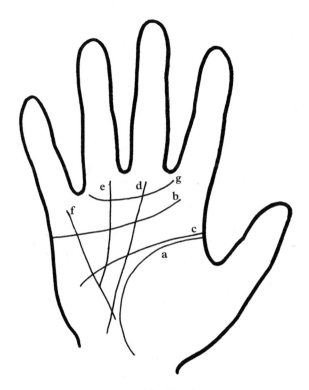

Figure 16.1: The Major Lines of the Hand

a. Atma rekha   d. Indira rekha   g. Mandoshnada
b. Bandha rekha   e. Kamala rekha   rekha
c. Dhan rekha   f. Bala rekha

319

Figure 16.2: Atma rekha beginning at Mani Bandha rekha

Figure 16.3: Atma rekha "ending" at base of index finger

If it moves right into the base of the index finger (Figure 16.3), the person is destined to live at least a hundred years.

If this lines contains a branch running up towards the *Pithru sthana* (Figure 16.4), the person will attain a high position in his or her chosen profession.

If a small dot appears on

Figure 16.4: Branch from Atma rekha towards Pithru sthana

320

this line, it foretells the birth of a son at the age where the dot appears. However, if the dot is black in color, the person will be involved in a scandal.

When found on a woman's hand, a small star formation at the end of this line indicates widowhood.

Bandha Rekha
(Ayu Rekha)

Bandha rekha (Figure 16.1b) corresponds to the heart line in Western palmistry. While in the West the line is said to begin at the percussion of the hand under the mount of Mercury and end near the Jupiter or Saturn finger, traditional Hindu palmists believe that this line ends under the *Jaya sthana* (mount of Mercury).

Although many modern Indian palmists believe that the characteristics and meanings of this line are similar to those of the West, traditional Hindu palmists teach that it is more like a life line or a "line of character."

The Sanskrit term *bandha* has to do with the Hindu concept of bondage, or life on this earth. When the heart line begins at the base of the index finger, ends at the percussion of the hand, and is free from breaks or color changes, Hindu palmists believe that the person will live for a hundred years.

Because *Bandha rekha* moves across the top of the hand, it

is believed to reflect the influences of several of the sthanas and thus affect the entire life. Generally speaking, the longer the line, the greater the potential for longevity.

Dhan Rekha (Matri rekha)

The Western head line is called *Dhan rekha,* "mother line," by the Hindus (Figure 16.1c). Like the head line, *Dhan rekha* reflects the mental processes, including reasoning ability, imagination, self-control, and clarity of mind.

Among the early Hindus, it was believed that the length and clarity of this line revealed one's potential wealth and material possessions, because the careful use of intelligence and reasoning powers would naturally lead to power, position, and economic abundance.

If this line is connected with the *Atma rekha* (Figure 16.5), Indian palmists consider that it is a sign of good fortune in that the person is likely to accumulate much property.

Figure 16.5: Dhan rekha connected to Atma rekha

- When found on either *Brathru sthana* or *Bandhu sthana*: unhappy marriage
- When located on *Satru sthana* (Figure 17.5): the individual is likely to suffer injury or death due to a quarrel or attack
- When found in the Lunar mount: danger of death by drowning
- When located at a point just above the *Bandha rekha* (Figure 17.6): danger of severe head injury
- When appearing on the third phalange of the middle finger (on a female hand): no children

Figure 17.5: Cross on Satru sthana

Figure 17.6: Cross above Bandha rekha

- When appearing on the top phalange of the little finger: poverty; life without a mate

Dots

As in Western palmistry, dots are usually an indicator of illness or accident. A reddish dot appearing on the *Bandha rekha* (Figure 17.7) would indicate a possible accident or injury involving the head; a yellowish dot on the *Atma rekha* would be a sign of liver disease at the age (approximately) where it appears on the line.

A dot appearing at the end of a line would reveal a sudden or catastrophic end to the qualities the line represents: if found at the end of *Indira rekha*, for example, the profession might end in

Figure 17.7: Dot on Bandha rekha

disaster or the person might lose his or her wealth. If appearing at the end of a marriage line, the marriage would end suddenly due to death or scandal.

The Fish

This curious symbol is found above the wrist (Figure 17.8). Its presence on the hand reveals prosperity and good fortune. It is often found on the hand of a person who is likely to have a major leadership role in his or her community, and who is known for benevolence and charity towards others.

The Flag

The presence of this rare mark (Figure 17.9) anywhere on the palm is considered a sign of moral courage and purity

Figure 17.8: The Fish

Figure 17.9: The Flag

of character. It is sometimes found on the hands of wealthy and influential individuals who are admired and respected in the community.

The Grille

As in the West, the grille is considered an unfortunate sign. Its presence tends to diminish the positive qualities of the *sthana* on which it appears.

- If located on the *Pithru sthana* (Figure 17.10): tends to be egotistical, domineering, and stubborn

- If found on the *Mathru sthana*: prone to depression and melancholy

- A grille on the *Vidya sthana*: sign of a superstitious nature

- If appearing on the *Jaya sthana*: the person cannot be trusted

- A grille on the *Dharma sthana*: sign of sudden, premature death

Figure 17.10: Grille on Pithru sthana

- If appearing on the Mount of Luna: suicidal tendencies

The Island

The island is considered an unfortunate sign in Hindu palmistry, because it indicates periods of weakness or misfortune wherever it appears on a line.

- An island on a *Jaya rekha* (marriage line), for example (Figure 17.11): major problems in the person's primary relationship

- Islands on the *Indira rekha*: serious reversals in career or finances; loss of wealth through sexual intrigue

- Islands on the *Bandha rekha*: adulterous affairs; if the *Pithru sthana* is large and fleshy: heart disease

- An island located at the end of a line: the person will end his or her days in misery

Figure 17.11: Island on Jaya rekha

The Moon

The Moon (Figure 17.12) is a sign of a kind individual with a gentle disposition wherever it is found on the palm. Hindu palmists teach that those with this rare mark are loved and admired by large numbers of people.

Figure 17.12: The Moon

The Square

As in other palmistry schools, the Hindus teach that the square is a sign of protection and preservation that tends to cancel out the negative connotations of any broken or split lines in the hand. If covering a break on the *Indira rekha*, for example (Figure 17.13), a square would save its owner from a severe business reversal or other career setback.

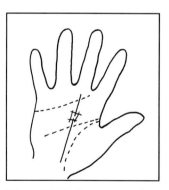

Figure 17.13: Square covering break on line

- Appearing on *Brathru sthana* (Figure 17.14): person will be an authority in religion or philosophy
- A star within a square on *Mathru sthana* (Figure 17.15): protection from murder

The Star

The star is made up of either three or six tiny lines forming a star-like pattern. Though usually considered a favorable sign, its meaning varies according to its clarity and its location on the hand. Generally speaking, a star is believed to indicate a situation that one cannot easily change.

Figure 17.14: Square on Brathru sthana

Figure 17.15: Star within a square

357

- When found at the end of the *Atma rekha* (Figure 17.16): person will achieve greatness due to his or her intellectual abilities

- When located on the *Atma rekha* itself: danger of accident at the age where the star appears

- When found on the *Mathra sthana* on a hand with clear, strong lines (Figure 17.17): high attainment in life

- When found on the *Mathra sthana* on a hand with poor lines: homicidal tendencies

- When located on the *Vidya sthana*: great wealth, fame, and high reputation

- When found on the *Jaya sthana*: untrustworthy; thief

Figure 17.16: Star at the end of Atma rekha

Figure 17.17: Star on Mathra sthana

- When found on the *Dharma sthana*: fame and accomplishment due to one's own tenacity. If found on both hands: suicidal

- When located on the *Brathru sthana*: major conquests in love and relationships

- When found in the center of the palm: sign of premature death surrounded by great publicity

The Sword

Also known as *Kuthar rekha*, the Sword (Figure 17.18) has significance only when found on the *Vidya sthana*. Considered an unlucky sign, its presence indicates that the person's life will be one of struggle and challenge.

Figure 17.18: The Sword

The Temple

A rare marking, the Temple (Figure 17.19) is occasionally found on the hands of a person occupying a very high position in society, such as a multi-millionaire or a member of royalty. Also found among noted scholars, religious leaders, and accomplished writers, it is considered a sign that the individual will reach the heights of his or her profession or station in life.

Figure 17.19: The Temple

The Tree

The Tree is often formed at the end of another line (Figure 17.20), though it can also involve the small lines that emanate upwards from a line (Figure 17.21). The presence of a tree is considered very positive by Hindu palmists, especially when found at the end of *Indira rekha, Atma rekha, Bandha rekha,* and *Kamala rekha,* on the lines of Fate, Life, Head, or Apollo. Depending on where it is found, the Tree enhances the positive aspects

Figure 17.20: The Tree at the end of a line

360

of a line, and strengthens the potential for longevity, fame, wealth, brilliance, or happiness.

The Triangle

Triangles can be either small or large. They are formed by three small independent lines or several larger ones. In Hindu palmistry, a small triangle found on the *Bandha rekha* (Figure 17.22) reveals an individual who will enjoy success through his or her own efforts. When found on either the *Dhan rekha* or the head line, it is a sign that the person will come into an inheritance.

Triangles located on the different *sthana*s have the following meanings:

* On *Pithru sthana*

Figure 17.21: The Tree rising from a line

Figure 17.22: Small triangle on Bandha rekha

(Figure 17.23): skilled at diplomacy

- On *Mathra sthana*: attracted to mysticism; talented in occult sciences

- On *Vidya sthana*: strong talent in art and design

- On *Jaya sthana*: ability as a diplomat

- On *Dharma sthana*: talent in the martial arts

Figure 17.23: Triangle on Pithru sthana

- On *Brathru* or *Bandhu sthana*: person falls deeply in love with his or her mate

The Trident

Like the tree mentioned earlier, the Trident can appear either independently (Figure 17.24) or at the end of another line (Figure 17.25). Considered rare by Indian palmists, it is a sign of good fortune.

- When found on the *Pithru sthana* (Figure 17.24): the person will achieve his or her aspirations in life.

Figure 17.24: Trident at end of Kamala rekha on Vidya sthana

Figure 17.25: Trident on Pithru sthana

- When located on the *Vidya sthana* (Figure 17.25): a high degree of celebrity and renown

Yav

Taking the form of a small oval, *yav* (or *yava*) can be found on the lower phalange of the thumb, on the *Mani-Bandha rekha* (Rascettes of Venus), on the joints of the fingers, and at the beginning or end of certain lines. Its appearance is not unlike a large island when found on a line.

Figure 17.26: Yav on lower phalange of thumb

Figure 17.27: Yav at base of the thumb

Figure 17.28: Yav at beginning of Indira rekha

Figure 17.29: Yav at end of Bandha rekha

- If found on the lower phalange of the thumb (Figure 17.26): material wealth and overall success in life
- If located at the base of the thumb (Figure 17.27): the person will have a son.
- If found at the beginning of *Indira rekha* (Figure 17.28): death of parents at an early age
- If located at the end of *Bandha rekha* (Figure 17.29): the person will die at a holy place (such as in Varanasi, one of the holiest cities in India).

IV

CHINESE PALMISTRY

Like the Hindus, the Chinese have been studying hands for literally thousands of years. Archeologists have uncovered evidence of ancient texts that reveal that palmistry was practiced in China as far back as the Zhou Dynasty (11th century B.C.–775 B.C.). Its popularity grew during the Spring and Autumn Period (770–475 B.C.) and the Warring States Period (475–221 B.C.), when palmists were held in high esteem for their ability to read character and future. Medical palmistry also developed during that time, but reached its maturity during the Ming Dynasty, which lasted from 1368 to 1644 A.D.

Early Chinese philosophers taught that each human being is a reflection of the universe and that the universe is a reflection of human beings. By understanding human beings, we can understand the universe. Palmistry in China was originally a spiritual study dedicated to understanding the mysteries of existence.

The ancient art and science of *xiang jenn,* or "the study of man," involves careful observation of a person's physical characteristics, such as the ears, face, feet, and body type, which are believed to reveal not only one's all-important family history, but an individual's psychological traits, spiritual potential, physical health, career and marriage possibilities, and the overall type of existence he or she will be likely to lead. Chinese palmistry, known as *xiang cheou* ("hand appearances"), is part of this ancient tradition, and, like astrology, is extremely popular among the Chinese. Many traditional Chinese doctors still examine the hand carefully in order to arrive at a thorough medical diagnosis.

Like Western palmistry, Chinese palmistry focuses on basic hand types, as well as the fingers, mounts, and lines that make up the human hand. It is also imiportant to evaluate skin texture, temperature, flexibility, and hand size. Special attention is given to a wide variety of small markings, whose significance often varies according to their location on the hand. While space limitations do not allow a complete discussion on this ancient art and science, the following pages will provide a basic introduction to this fascinating study.

18

HAND TYPES
AND PALM
CHARACTERISTICS

Early Chinese fortune tellers believed that a person's entire life could be seen in the palm, and they would read it in great detail. However, like practitioners from other schools of palmistry, they taught that the meanings of certain lines in the palm are modified by features of the fingers, nails, and the hand as a whole, as described in earlier sections of this book.

Hand Types

There are five elemental types of hand in Chinese Palmistry. While their qualities correspond with some of the traditional

Western hand types, hands are classified according to the five elements: Earth, Fire, Metal, Wood, and Water.

The Five Elements theory compares the human body to a small universe. The sequence of creation follows a uniform pattern of water-wood-fire-earth-metal-water. According to a Chinese medical text: "Where there is water, trees grow; friction on wood produces fire; fire turns the wood back to earth; the earth crystallized becomes metal; and metal in contact with cold forms water." Although all human beings are composed of these five elements, it is believed that each individual has a specific "keynote" element that is reflected in his or her hands.

Like other aspects of traditional Chinese fortune-telling and character analysis, many beliefs surrounding palmistry reflect traditional Chinese culture, with its reverence for ancestors, strict observance of class divisions, strong belief in the inevitability of destiny, and a distinct favoritism towards males in the family.

For example, a simian line on a woman's hand is considered very unlucky in Chinese palmistry, because it is believed to indicate that she is destined for a life of misfortune, challenge, and hard work. Like most Chinese women, a prospective bride with such a hand would be involved in an arranged marriage. Since she would likely have her hand read by a palmist before her engagement, certain observations and expectations would be made regarding her future as a wife; as a result, her marriage situation might well be determined on the reading itself. Having been classified as a poor marriage prospect because she has a simian line in her hand, her chances of a marrying a suitable husband are less promising than a women whose hands have the normal head line/heart line configuration. As a result, her life could indeed become one of suffering and toil, as she fulfills the prediction of having an "unlucky" hand.

In Western palmistry, a simian line on a woman's hand reveals tenacity and a love of work; a woman with such a line could not only successfully manage a farm and raise a large family (even if her husband were not present), but could also be an outstanding executive or entrepreneur. This more enlightened analysis may encourage a young woman with a simian line in her hand to pursue advanced studies and to use her energy and tenacity to achieve a fulfilling career. Although "lots of work" would be a part of her life, it would be a positive and satisfying aspect rather than a negative one. While observing the spirit of the early teachers, we have taken the liberty of offering more modern interpretations of many old beliefs.

Earth Hands

Like elementary hands in the Western palmistry tradition, short, stubby fingers and a squarish palm indicate "earthy" qualities (Figure 18.1). Earth hands are often fleshy and contain only the major lines. People with earth hands are usually slow-moving, stable, and reliable, enjoying living and working close to the land.

However, this type of hand is not considered lucky, since it is believed that its owners often show minimal success despite years of hard work. This belief often reflects the traditional life of a Chinese peasant, who is still considered at the bottom of the social and economic scale in China today.

Figure 18.1: Earth Hand

Fire Hands

In Chinese palmistry, fire hands tend to be large, with delicate, long tapering fingers (Figure 18.2). In some ways they resemble a combination of conic hand and psychic hand characteristics

Figure 18.2: Fire Hand

in Western palmistry. These hands also may contain an abundance of small lines. People with these hands would be sensitive and impressionable, and are likely to be very creative. Though full of energy, they may lack the strength and tenacity of a person with a different kind of hand.

Like those people with earth hands, owners of fire hands are not considered fortunate, because their hard work produces only middling results.

Metal Hands

Metal hands are well-proportioned, the fingers the same general length as the palm, which tends to be roundish. The fingers and skin texture are usually smooth and contain few lines. The primary distinguishing feature of these hands are three horizontal lines defining each of the finger joints (Figure 18.3).

Figure 18.3: Metal Hand

This type of hand is considered the best to have, and overall good fortune will invariably come to the owner through little effort. However, the presence of individual signs in the hand (discussed later on) can offer specific information regarding special accomplishments, honors, and wealth.

Wood Hands

Wood hands are well proportioned, with a squarish palm and strong, nicely formed fingers. However, the index or Jupiter finger tends to predominate, and the hands are usually firm in texture. The skin is generally dry and the hand contains many small lines, especially vertical lines found on the various phalanges of the fingers and on the mounts of Venus and Luna (Figure 18.4). Vertical lines tend to indicate strong energy, and a strong Jupiter finger reflects an assertive, dynamic nature.

This hand is not considered as lucky as the metal hand. Its owners can achieve success only after a great deal of effort, even with the presence of special palmar markings.

Figure 18.4: Wood Hand

Water Hands

The water hand (Figure 18.5) is usually roundish and characterized by overall puffiness, especially in the third and second phalanges of the fingers. Such hands would likely be soft and bland to the touch, although they would not necessarily be flabby and thick. The owners of these hands tend to love luxury and are not interested in hard work. As you can imagine, owners of

Figure 18.5: Water hand

water hands are generally viewed as unlucky by Chinese palmists, and not likely to achieve success in life.

Palm Characteristics

Size of the Palm and Fingers

As in Western palmistry, the Chinese measure the size of the hand in relation to the person's overall body size. In addition, remember that in Chinese palmistry, finger length is determined by the length of the middle finger compared to the palm; ideally, the palm and the middle finger should be the same length.

- A large hand on a person with a relatively small body: happiness and success
- Small hands and a large body: poverty
- If you place your arms at your sides and your hands do not reach your thighs: a life of poverty
- If your arms and hands reach past the region where the thighs begin: wisdom
- Long palm, short fingers: scandal without reason
- Long palm, short, thin fingers: person abandons his or her fortune
- Palm and fingers of equal length, fingers slender and well-formed: unable to achieve success
- Small person, large palm: money-oriented
- Flabby palm: coarse, crude individual
- Flabby hand on thin person: harmony in life
- Flabby hand on fat person: no special meaning
- Large, thick palm: person will be appreciated by others
- Short, well-formed palm: natural humility
- Flat palm on delicate hand: weak body
- Rounded palm with hard consistency: lacks intelligence

- Presence of prominent mounts on the palm: special abilities
- Presence of prominent mounts plus a marked depression in the center of the palm: wealth and riches
- Presence of prominent mounts and flat center of the palm: money inherited or earned will likely be wasted

Consistency

- Fleshy hands: ability to make money
- Bony hands: difficulty making money
- Muscular hands: strength; one's efforts bring good fortune
- Hard hand: stupidity

People who grab your hand forcefully, causing pain, are considered by the Chinese to be stupid, slow-witted, and vulgar.

Palm Color

The ancient Chinese placed great emphasis on the color of the palm. Remember that because the skin color of an average

Chinese person will be slightly different from that of a person of Anglo-Saxon background, for example, the skin color meanings described here are particular to the Chinese.

- Reddish palms: owner will be proud and appreciated by others; honors and high position result.
- When a pregnant woman has a reddish palm with violet tints and large nails, she will give birth to a son.
- When a pregnant woman has a greyish palm, she will give birth to a daughter.
- Light bluish color: fearless and worry-free personality
- Light bluish color on the mounts of the hand: good health
- Dark bluish color: misfortune
- Whitish color: omen of a lifetime of many sorrows
- Light yellow: happiness and honors
- Dark yellow palms: omen of misfortune and death

Temperature

In Chinese palmistry, the temperature of the hand should ideally follow the seasons. It should be warm in the summer, cool and dry during the winter, and slightly warm in the spring.

However, if the hand is cold even during the summer, it is

considered a sign of poor health and misfortune in life. If the hand is dry and cool in the summer and hot in the winter, it is a sign of stupidity and ignorance. In general, cold hands are a sign that the individual will not enjoy a prosperous life and will have to struggle to maintain a comfortable standard of living, especially if the hand is dry as well.

A warm and humid hand has long been considered a sign that the person will be wealthy and respected by others, but a very warm hand indicates nervous excitation and fever.

Skin Texture

In general, skin texture reflects fortune and riches.

- Smooth, fine skin on a firm hand: abundance and purity
- Smooth, fine skin on a strong man's hand: good fortune and high position
- Smooth, fine skin on a flabby or weak hand: poverty

Skin Color

Skin color is considered on both the palm and the back of the hand. Ideally, both the palm and the back of the hand should be the same color.

- Both palm and back having the same pink color:

good health and excellent fortune

- Back of the hand darker than the palm: great wealth
- Back of the hand lighter than the palm: poverty

If the back of the hand is

- white and transparent: indifferent personality
- white and bland: dull personality
- pink with veins: benevolence
- reddish: poor health
- reddish purple: lazy; poor health
- brownish with rosy coloring: good health; pleasing character

19

THE NINE PALACES

As in other schools of palmistry, early Chinese hand readers placed great importance on specific regions of the palm. The Chinese named them "palaces." The nine palaces are made up of eight mounts (known as *koa*) plus the "Audience Chamber" or "Reception Hall" (the room where important guests are received), which is located at the center of the palm.

Palace of the Wind (Siuann kong)

The Palace of the Wind is made up of what we know as the mount of Jupiter and the muscle located between the index and middle fingers (Figure 19.1a). Also known as the Door of Metal and the Peak of Valor, it corresponds to the first 25 years of a person's life.

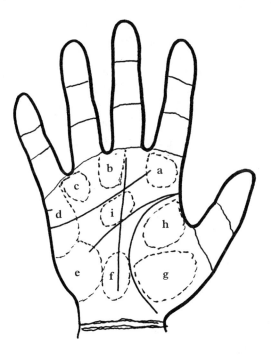

Figure 19.1: The Nine Palaces

a- The Palace of the Wind
b- The Palace of Separation
c- The Palace of Earth
d- The Palace of Happiness
e- The Palace of the Sky

f- The Palace of the Pit
g- The Mountain Palace
h- The Palace of Lightning
i- The Reception Hall

In China, wind is an ancient symbol of power and moveable boundaries. The more elevated the mount, the greater the possibility of achieving the power that comes from wealth. Chinese sages recognized that we grasp and hold on to objects primarily with our thumb and index finger: so, this mount corresponds to both the real and symbolic power located in this part of the hand.

- If well-developed: wealth and being surrounded by employees and others who assist them in carrying out their duties

- If deficient: submission to the will of others; unable to be successful in life

- If highly elevated: good-natured

- If the mount extends lower towards the center of the palm: the person will likely "drift" in life, and not find happiness in his or her career and relationship.

The Palace of Separation (Li kong)

Known as the Summer Palace and the Peak of Earnings (emoluments), this region traditionally is connected to summer, and corresponds to ages 25–50 in a person's life (Figure 19.1b). It is made up of the muscular eminence between the middle and ring fingers, which often extends to what we call the heart line. Basically speaking, this region corresponds to all that is beautiful and elegant. In earlier times, it governed official appointments and tasks, travel, and separation from friends and family. Although the life of a modern business executive and a government diplomat is very different from the kind of service done by a Chinese government official ten centuries ago, many of the old-fashioned meanings related to this mount can apply today.

In ancient China, official appointments were a sign of power and prestige, not only for the individual appointee, but for his entire family. However, they often involved moving from province to province with frequent separations from family and friends. The more this mount is elevated, the greater the chances for achieving respect and renown as a government official.

- If elevated: likely to receive honors while in government service or as a scholar

- If elevated and coming to a point: shall receive official appointments and will work as a government official

- If vertical lines are etched on this region: good fortune, awards, and recognition. The person is apt to be better known than his or her ancestors

- Large in size: if on the hands of a civil servant, long employment; if on the hands of a soldier, promotions and awards

- Weak or deficient: recognition and honors that are quickly forgotten by others

Figure 19.2: The Net on Palace of Separation

Figure 19.3: The Well on Palace of Separation

- Sign of the Net on this mount (Figure 19.2): destined to be a high government official
- Sign of the Well on this mount (Figure 19.3): appointment to the Emperor's court, which in modern times could indicate promotion to a Board of Directors of a company

The Palace of Earth (Kroun kong)

Consisting of the elevation between the ring and little fingers (Figure 19.1c), this region resonates with Earth energy, fertility, and reproduction. It is also known as the Door of the Earth and the Peak of Happiness. This region represents beauty, and all that is pleasant and agreeable to the senses. It corresponds to ages 50 to 75.

In centuries past, the Chinese believed that the Earth nourishes humanity—with air, water, shelter and food—without humans having to ask for anything. The stronger and more prominent this region, the greater the chances are for achieving success in life without having to fight for it.

- If this palace is developed: happiness for women and good relations with one's children in the later years
- If flat: one's daughters will grow old prematurely
- If sunken: one's marriage would be ruined by scandals
- If pinkish in color and warm to the touch: good health and few sorrows through old age
- If yellowish and cold to the touch: many erotic dreams
- If the palace contains the Chinese word for "ten" (Figure 19.4): a peaceful life and wealth due to a powerful benefactor
- If the palace contains a circle ("Buddha's Eye") (Figure 19.5): the person will achieve success through his or her own efforts
- If the palace contains the word for "woman" (Figure 19.6): wealth
- If the palace contains the Sign of the Fishes (Figure 19.7): honors from altruistic deeds

Figure 19:4: The word for "Ten" on Palace of Earth

Figure 19.5: The Buddha's Eye on Palace of Earth

Figure 19.6: The word "Woman" on Palace of Happiness

Figure 19.7: Sign of the Fishes on Palace of Happiness

The Palace of Happiness (Toe kong)

The Palace of Happiness (also known as the Palace of Wives and Favorite Mistresses) is located in a part of the hand that corresponds to the Upper Mount of Mars and extends to the lower part of the Mount of Mercury (Figure 19.1d). Related to the season of autumn, it signifies the presence of primary partners and lovers, which usually meant wives and mistresses in early China. Today, of course, it may include the boyfriends or girlfriends of a person of either sex, both inside and outside of marriage.

In earlier times, a loving wife and beautiful mistresses were considered primary sources of pleasure for a Chinese man, while a good husband and at least several children were the main sources of happiness for a woman. These criteria have changed somewhat over the centuries, but the spirit of their meaning is the same. The height of this mount determines the intensity of the satisfaction that these individuals bring to one's life.

- If strong, becoming more elevated towards the upper part of the region: sweet and kind disposition

- If weak and shallow with horizontal lines: servants will not remain in the person's service for long. Today this may mean that the domestic life will be stormy and unstable

- Lesions on this area: abandonment by one's mate
- Presence of the word for "woman" on this region: the presence of a benefactor in one's life
- Single line ("line of a single species") across the percussion of this region (Figure 19.8): homosexuality

Figure 19.8: Line of a Single Species

The Palace of the Sky (Tsienn kong)

This region corresponds with the mount of Luna (Figure 19.1e) It signifies the sky, continuous movement, and the Lord who shares His gifts. It is also known as the Palace of the Father and the Son. In ancient China, the sky is viewed as hidden protection, as is the influence of a father who quietly teaches his children proper conduct and thus protects them from danger.

Even in modern Chinese communities, the firstborn son holds the highest status of all the siblings. He is destined to receive his parents' inheritance, even if he has older sisters and other siblings. If his father should die, he assumes the honorary role of the "father" in the family structure, even if he is still a teenager. Being a firstborn son, he has other burdens as well. If a firstborn son does not marry and have children of his own, he is considered a disgrace to his family—and by extension, to all of his ancestors—because he is not passing along the family name. Although this old model is beginning to change, the importance of having a son (especially a firstborn son) cannot be underestimated.

For these reasons, the Palace of the Sky is believed to reveal the success of one's descendants, the ability to foretell the future, and overall success in life.

- If the summit of the region is located towards the Palace of Happiness: triumph for the firstborn son

- A strong mount that contains lines or other markings: nobility for one's descendants

- If the region is elevated: long life and the wisdom to overcome life's obstacles

- The presence of a square ("Seal of Gold") (Figure 19.9): great wisdom

The Palace of the Pit (Krann kong)

The Palace of the Pit is located at the base of the hand

between the mounts of Venus and Luna; the destiny or fate line often begins here (Figure 19.1f). It is associated with the winter season and with water, which flows down from the mountains and collects naturally and effortlessly in a pit or large hole. This signifies the material wealth and hereditary talents that are given by one's ancestors.

Figure 19.9: Seal of Gold on Palace of the Sky

Also known as the Palace of Water or the Door to the Sea, this palace governs not only our potential for material wealth, but also the level of esteem for our parents, the strength of ancestral values, and our inherited talents and abilities. The larger and more well-formed this region, the greater the chances of inheriting both material and spiritual wealth from one's ancestors.

- If elevated: hidden protection from one's ancestors

- When thick and containing markings: the potential to achieve nobility

- When weak and indented, and containing random lines: the person will be disgraced by either his or her own actions or the actions of others

- If divided by a line that moves up the hand (such as the fate line or the "Jade Column" in Chinese palmistry): appreciation and respect
- If the region contains numerous vertical lines "like silk threads" (Figure 19.10): success in one's endeavors
- When a line comes from the Palace of the Mountain (the lower part of the mount of Venus) and moves into this region in the form of a hook (Figure 19.11): the individual will receive the approval and support of his or her ancestors
- When a line, moving from the Palace of the Mountain into the Palace of the Pit, has three

Figure 19.10: Small vertical lines on Palace of the Pit

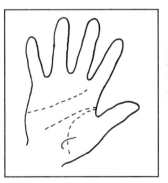

Figure 19.11: A hooked line on Palace of the Pit

branches (Figure 19.12): three changes of residence, without our ancestors abandoning us (in early China, most sons continued to live in the ancestral home, even after they married, so moving from house to house or city to city was relatively rare)

- When there are gaps in the lines: the individual will receive help from another person
- A triangle: possible victim of robbery
- The presence of the "Kittens of the Willow" (Figure 19.13): a generation of honors and wealth

Figure 19.12: A line with three branches

Figure 19.13: Kittens of the Willow

The Mountain Palace (Kenn kong)

This palace is composed of what we call the lower mount of Venus (Figure 19.1g). It is also known as the Door of Wood and the Palace of Brothers and Sisters. In ancient China as today, the integrity of the family unit was extremely important, and a harmonious relationship between brothers and sisters was highly desirable. In Chinese philosophy, mountains represent obstacles and challenges, but they also signify protection from invaders. In a sense, friends and siblings may question our decisions and prevent us from doing whatever we want, but they also provide us with mutual protection and support during our lifetime.

According to tradition, this region of the hand concerns harmony and understanding between ourselves and our siblings. It is also the repository of an individual's wealth and possessions, as well as family homes and ancestral tombs.

- If weak or deficient: problems with parents and siblings early in life

- If the area contains numerous vertical lines (Figure 19.14): the siblings and the family will live far away from each other and there will be many separations. It also can signify that the person will spend much time alone or will live without family support

- If this mount contains a grille (Figure 19.15): melan-

Figure 19.14: Vertical lines on
Mountain Palace

Figure 19.15: Grille on
Mountain Palace

choly and boredom with life can easily occur if the
person does not have a stable career

h. *Palace of Lightning (Tchenn kong)*

Located in what Westerners call the upper mount of Venus
(Figure 19.1h), this palace is ruled by thunder, or "that
which causes commotion." It is also connected to spring,
the season of instability and atmospheric disturbances. For
these reasons Chinese sages believed that this region is connected to the excitation of amorous feelings, which lead us
to choose lovers and life partners. As in Western palmistry,

this region indicates our basic level of energy as it relates to sexual interest, but it also reveals our capacity for using this energy in work and other nonsexual activities.

- If elevated: the individual will acquire enough property to take care of a generation of descendants
- If elevated in a woman's hand: she will be in charge of the family wealth, or assured of "great happiness" in general
- If weak or sunken, with many horizontal lines across the mount: lack of wealth and lack of friendship among children
- If vertical lines are present, family wealth is threatened

Figure 19.16: Lines of Libertine Desires

Figure 19.17: Sign of the Well in Palace of Lightning

- The presence of the "Lines of Libertine Desires" (Figure 19.16): many love affairs

- The presence of the "Sign of the Well" (Figure 19.17): the accumulation of a large amount of real estate

The Reception Hall (Ming trang)

Also known as the "Hall of Clarity," this palace is located in the center of the palm between what we call the head line and the heart line (Figure 19.1i).

This area, seemingly protected by the other regions of the hand, is believed to guide one's life. It governs energy, riches, and overall abundance, and reveals the potential for both good luck and misfortune. It is known as the Hall of Clarity, because one's good fortune and respectability are determined by one's own mental clarity, which leads to making correct judgments and having order and discipline in life.

- If this area is dark: disgrace in life is certain

- If red and somewhat greasy: great happiness is assured

- If this area contains many squares (Figure 19.18): good fortune

- The presence of a circle, or "the Eye" (Figure 19.19): mystical temperament, with interest in medi-

Figure 19.18: Squares within the Reception Hall

Figure 19.19: The Eye in the Reception Hall

Figure 19.20: The Jade Stairway in the Reception Hall

Figure 19.21: The Southern Star in the Reception Hall

tation, occult sciences, and mysticism

- The presence of "The Well": happiness and high honors
- The presence of "The Jade Stairway" (Figure 19.20): the probability of receiving high grades on examinations; by extension, it also is a sign that the person will eventually become successful and wealthy

Figure 19.22: The Rope in the Reception Hall

- The presence of "The Southern Star" (Figure 19.21): the individual will eventually wield power over much territory
- The presence of "The Rope" (Figure 19.22): one of the worst signs one can have: it indicates hanging.

Other Regions of the Hand

In addition to the Nine Palaces, other regions of less importance can be found on the hand.

Figure 19.23: Properties and Houses

Figure 19.24: Good Salaries

The region of Property and Houses, or *tienn che*, is a muscular eminence found on the edge of the Palace of Lightning (Figure 19.23). In physical terms, this region is connected to the thumb's ability to grasp and hold onto things. If this part of the hand is strong and dominated by lightning, chances are good that the person will acquire money and real estate.

Good Salaries (Figure 19.24) is composed of a small triangle formed by three lines of the hand: the Line of Man (head line), the Jade Column (fate line), and what we call the line of Mercury. If this triangle is clear and well-formed, it indicates control over the emotions (an important trait among traditional Chinese), which leads to overall success in life.

The Palaces Together

In addition to the individual significance of each palace, Chinese sages taught the importance of the relationship among various palaces.

The Three Guests

The Three Guests or the Three Marvels are made up of the three palaces found under the fingers: Wind, Separation, and Earth.

As mentioned before, the fuller and more elevated the mount, the greater the potential for wealth, happiness, and success during the time of life represented by the mount. If, for example, the Palace of the Earth is very large and elevated, it indicates the potential to enjoy wealth, happiness, and good fortune in one's later years. Weak, absent, or indented mounts reveal the potential for failure and misfortune.

However, our way of thinking and feeling can change a deficient mount. Happiness is believed to actually increase the size of these palaces.

There is no special interpretation for differing sizes and elevations of these mounts when considered as a group.

The Four Seasons

The Four Seasons are made up of the palaces of Lightning (spring), Separation (summer), Happiness (autumn), and Pit (winter).

Ideally, all four mounts should be large and full. If they are not of comparable size, it indicates that one's life will be plagued by obstacles and instability, bringing about misfortune.

If one palace dominates the others, there will be an excess of energy in that area of life. For example, if the Palace of Lightning is overly large in comparison to the others, the person will be obsessed with pursuing sexual pleasure. If the Palace of Separation dominates, blind ambition will rule the personality at the expense of other aspects of life, such as concern for family.

The Four Doors

The Four Doors are made up of the palaces of Wind, Earth, Sky, and Mountain. As with the Four Seasons, a lack of harmony in the size and strength of these mounts will bring about suffering and bitterness in life.

20

FINGERS AND NAILS

The fingers have long held special importance among the Chinese, because they are considered a sure sign of a person's intellectual and spiritual evolution. Long, tapered, and graceful fingers have always been recognized in China as the sign of a sensitive and cultivated individual, while short, bulky fingers have long been considered a sign of a coarse, boorish person with limited intellectual gifts.

Unlike many Western cultures, traditional Chinese society follows the ancient precept of "proper relationship," which was introduced by the great sage Confucius (551–479 B.C.). He taught that there are five fundamental human relationships that are essential to a stable society: between husband and wife, between parents and children, between siblings, between the Emperor and his subjects, and finally, between friends.

Some early Chinese palmistry texts teach that the thumb and four fingers symbolize one's family, considered the all-important social unit among the Chinese for thousands of years. Reverence for one's ancestors remains an essential aspect of Chinese life today, and, as we have seen, passing on the family name to future generations is considered an obligation of firstborn sons. As a reflection of this ancient belief, the thumb in Chinese palmistry symbolizes our parents, the index finger stands for siblings, the middle finger is oneself, the ring finger stands for our mate, and the little finger represents our descendants. To the degree that these individual fingers are strong, supple, and well-formed, containing lines and other markings that symbolize positive aspects, they reflect well on these important people in our life.

Finger Characteristics

In Chinese palmistry, the relative size of the fingers in relation to the palm is of particular importance because it reflects the ancient Taoist concept of *balance*. The standard for measuring the fingers is the size of the middle finger; fingers longer than the palm are considered long, while those shorter than the palm are viewed as short.

Length

- Long: a sign of superior intelligence and the ability to make money
- Long and narrow: above average overall abilities and highly penetrating mind
- Long and tapered: refined and highly cultured
- Horizontal lines on long fingers: scorned by others
- Short: subject to criticism
- Short and stubby: low intelligence; unsuccessful in life

The Individual Fingers

The Thumb

In Chinese medicine, the thumb reveals our hereditary constitution. A person with a thumb that is both firm and long has a strong constitution, with good health, energy, and resistance to disease.

People with weak, supple thumbs, or thumbs that tend to be flat at the tip, are likely to be vulnerable to disease. They are often high-strung and suffer from nervous disorders, such as tension headaches and insomnia. Those whose thumbs are excessively stiff have a higher energy level than those with supple thumbs, but are more prone to migraine headaches and heart trouble.

The Index Finger

The index finger is viewed by Chinese physicians as a mirror of one's liver function, which is considered the most important organ of the body. The liver is the only organ (except the brain) that can perform over 500 specialized functions simultaneously, such as processing nutrients, cleansing the body of foreign substances, and storing essential nutrients for the body's use.

The Chinese believe that a strong and well-formed index finger is a sign of good liver function, especially if the finger is straight. A short, weak, thin or bent index finger is a sure sign of deficient liver function with accompanying fatigue; it can also be a sign of a poorly functioning digestive system.

The Middle Finger

The middle finger is believed to reflect the state of the body's circulatory system. A strong, straight middle finger that enjoys a slight degree of elasticity is a sign of good overall circulation. A finger that is crooked is a sign of poor circulation as well as deficient intestinal function. If the middle phalange is longer than the first and third phalanges, the person is likely to suffer from poor calcium metabolism, resulting in chronic problems with the bones and teeth.

The Ring Finger

Practitioners of Chinese medical palmistry believe that the ring finger reveals the person's overall state of health. A long, strong, and straight ring finger is a sign of a good constitution and a high level of health. If the finger is short (does not reach at least halfway up the top phalange of the middle finger), the person will be low in energy and susceptible to frequent bouts of disease. If the top phalange of the ring finger is thin, there may be problems with sexual function as well.

The middle phalange reflects the state of health of muscles and bones. The presence of small horizontal lines along the edge of this phalange reveals a potential for rheumatism, arthritis, and other bone-related problems.

The Little Finger

The little finger rules digestion. As with the other fingers of the hand, a long, straight, and strong little finger is a sign of good digestive function. Little fingers that are short, weak and/or crooked indicate that the person is subject to a wide variety of intestinal problems, especially indigestion, constipation, and parasites.

Comparing the Length of Individual Fingers

Among the early Chinese palmists, the index finger was known as the "host," and the ring finger was the "guest." Ideally, they should be roughly the same size when the fingers are together. When the host and the guest enjoy a good relationship, all goes well for the human being on whom these fingers are found!

- Index finger longer than ring finger: peaceful life; assured success
- Ring finger longer than index finger: modest life situation; difficulty in dealing with life's challenges
- Long little finger: appreciated by others; overcomes suffering and doubts; ability to overcome illness. The top of a long little finger reaches above the top joint of the ring finger.

Gaps between the Fingers

To analyze gaps between the fingers, the palm should be outstretched and the fingers held together. The gaps will be found between the lower phalanges of the fingers.

- Gap between index and middle fingers: detailed thinker; hates being dominated by others; considered a sign of good fortune
- Gap between middle and ring fingers: freedom–

loving; person lives in the moment and doesn't make plans for the future; very independent

- Gap between ring and little fingers: person does whatever he or she likes to do
- Gaps between all the fingers: open, optimistic personality; spends money easily
- No gaps between fingers: conservative in thinking and action; holds onto money and property

Form of the Fingers

- Knotted fingers: poor and needy throughout life
- Strong joints, strong bones: few pleasures in life with many problems
- Smooth fingers (like bamboo shoots): intelligence
- All ten fingers smooth and slender: tranquility in life; happiness
- Conic fingertips: much happiness
- Spatulate fingertips: indulging in foolish pursuits
- Index finger bending slightly towards middle finger: ear problems in youth
- Middle or ring finger bending towards each other: problems with the legs in middle age

- Little finger bending towards ring finger: low energy in old age
- Straight, stiff thumb: simple, uncomplicated person
- Supple thumb that arches back easily: difficulty finding satisfaction in life
- Thumb that does not arch back when held normally: won't give up easily

In Chinese philosophy, the thumb reflects basic intelligence as well as our reputation in the community. Intelligence governs perception, understanding, and realizing our dreams. The art of gaining respect and having influence over others is also connected to intelligence. For these reasons, the length, form, and balance between the two phalanges of the thumb are related to intelligence. Phalanges of equal length indicate strong intellect, although other aspects of the hand can modify this interpretation.

Lines and Markings on the Fingers (palm facing towards you)

The Chinese pay much attention to the lines that form the finger joints.

- Three lines on each finger joint: honors and wealth
- One line making up each finger joint (Figure 20.1):

laborer or other low-status occupation

- Absence of lines on any one of the finger joints: death by accident during a long trip

- Vertical lines on phalanges: favorable omen; good fortune in life

- Flat and weak vertical lines on phalanges: lowly position in life

Figure 20.1: One line on each finger joint

- Many vertical lines: favorable position in life; increased chances for advancement

- No vertical lines: unfavorable position in life; poor chances of high-status occupation

- When the lines pass through the joints (Figure 20.2): one's efforts are likely to result in failure.

Figure 20.2: Vertical lines passing through the joints

- Three horizontal lines at the base of the fingers: high social position with many opportunities for advancement; probability of having many employees
- One line at the base of each finger: low social position

The presence of certain "special" signs on the fingers will be discussed in a later chapter.

The Nails

The nails reflect a measure of our basic vitality, which includes energy, intelligence, the ability to adapt to the challenges of living, and even our potential length of life. For these reasons, the size, thickness, strength, and color of the nails are often used to predict the future.

Nail Length

- Long: audacious, likes to take risks in life; prone to respiratory problems
- Long and hard: very audacious
- Short: fear of taking risks; argumentative; prone to heart disease in men, gynecological problems in women
- Very long: person will suffer deceptions and illness;

tendency to begin too many projects and inability to complete them

Nail Shape

- Round: happiness and good fortune
- Pointed: intelligence and distinction
- Squarish: honest, clear thinker, ambitious; good health
- Strongly curved (Hippocratic nail): poor reasoning power
- Spoon nail: tendency towards hernias (men); if nail contains grooves: hemorrhoids
- Ridged at the tip: stupidity

Color and (Natural) Polish

- Shiny: abundance and wealth
- Yellowish-red: important situations will present themselves
- Yellowish and shiny: pure and high-minded friends and associates
- Reddish and flat: government employment

- Bluish yet shiny: faithful and loyal by nature
- Whitish and clear: laziness, irresponsibility
- Dark and clear: low status in life
- Half-moons on the nails: delicate constitution, low resistance to disease

Thickness and Hardness

- Firm and thick: long life
- Thick: longevity with many celebrations in your honor
- Hard and long: strong will and audacity; ability to understand situations easily
- Soft nails: laziness; fear of taking risks
- Soft and narrow: fear of taking risks; potential short life
- Soft and short: poor willpower; fear of taking risks; fear of beginning new projects

Dryness

- Dry nails indicate bad fortune and low overall capability
- Nails that break easily signify an inability to complete projects as well as trouble finishing projects correctly.

21

THE LINES OF
THE HANDS

The ancient Chinese believed that the lines of the human hand are not unlike the markings found in a piece of wood. When the wood contains a distinctive grain, it is considered both beautiful and valuable. By the same token, to the degree that the lines of the hand are both clearly and beautifully formed, they reveal an intelligent, sensitive, and kind person who is loved and appreciated by others.

Chinese palmists determine the timing of events on the lines as Western palmists do.

Generally speaking, lines in the hand are viewed as channels of energy for *chi*. The more abundant the number of well-formed lines in a person's hands, the greater the chances that the life will be filled with possibilities. By contrast, a person with three or four basic lines in the hand would have limited opportunities. However, an excessive number of small, diverse lines is also considered unfortunate, since they represent scattered energy and dilute the basic properties that individual lines represent. For this reason, both the *quality* and *quantity* of lines are important to the Chinese hand analyst. Some generalized qualities regarding the lines have been passed down through the generations:

- When lines cover the hand: sufficient food and clothing in later years
- Lines as close together as "threads on a ball of silk": happiness and wealth throughout old age
- When the lines of the hand are abundant and clear: long life is assured
- Numerous lines: a curious spirit
- Weak or absent lines: the owner will receive money without having to steal it
- Deep, clear lines: an open mind and an agreeable personality
- Small, weak lines: closed-minded view of life

Refined individuals possess hands with lines that are clear and well-defined; the lines form harmonious designs and the markings speak of good fortune. Coarse and unrefined people have hands with thick, heavy lines that are frequently broken or incomplete.

Studying the Lines

When a traditional Chinese hand analyst begins a consultation, he or she pays special attention to the clarity of the lines, as well as their depth, length, breaks, straightness, direction, and color. Some general interpretations follow:

Figure 21.1: Clear, well-formed lines

- Clearly defined lines: good health and overall good fortune

- Poorly defined lines: economic hardship throughout life

- Lines that are clear and well-formed (Figure

Figure 21.2: Wavy lines

21.1): solid, loyal, penetrating, and intelligent

- Wavy lines (Figure 21.2): two-faced, a natural cheater, who tends to be disloyal. People with such lines have difficulty following through with their plans
- Islands on the lines: loneliness, spiritual confusion
- Chained lines "like the knots on a whip" (Figure 21.3): difficulty in accomplishing tasks; easily deceived by others
- Forks at the end of a line (Figure 21.4): what you begin will be difficult to complete
- Lines that end with an island: death by drowning

Figure 21.3: Chained lines

Figure 21.4: Lines ending in a fork

- When all the major lines are chained and islanded at the end: poor self-expression; careless with words

- Lines that seem to cover the hand without having any particular direction: a life without focus

- Lines that are stopped by another line (Figure 21.5): difficulty reaching one's goals, especially in business or a vocation

- Small line cutting into a major line (Figure 21.6): known as "Nine Witches" in traditional Chinese palmistry, the presence of one or more of these lines indicates that others are trying to destroy your health, relationship, or business

Figure 21.5: Line stopped by another line

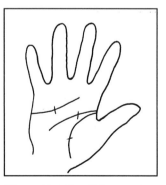

Figure 21.6: Small line cutting into major line

Figure 21.7: Gap in a major line

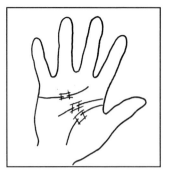

Figure 21.8: Square covering a gap on major line

- Gap in a major line (Figure 21.7): bankruptcy or other major loss. A life-threatening situation or death

- Square covering a gap in a major line (Figure 21.8): known as the "New Jade Line," this sign provides protection wherever it is found, and prevents misfortune

- Overlapping lines (Figure 21.9): recovery from misfortune; a seemingly unfortunate event will give rise to good fortune

- Double lines (Figure 21.10): this will make the single line "twice as strong"

- Branch leaving major line (Figure 21.11): known as

Figure 21.9: Overlapping lines

Figure 21.10: Double lines

Figure 21.11: Branch leaving
major line

Figure 21.12: Dots on a line

the "leaking line" by Chinese palmists, its presence
signifies the loss of money in business deals, through
gambling or lending money to others

- Dots on a major line (Figure 21.12): obstructions in
  life; loss, or illness

Length, Depth, and Color

- Deep lines: longevity, good fortune, happiness in
  old age
- Deeply marked broad lines: sign of a deep thinker;
  well-grounded
- Deep yet fine lines: good fortune
- Short and shallow lines: superficial personality; easily
  bored with life
- Thick and shallow lines: poor earning power
- Long and shallow lines: coarseness, impure character
- Lines that are barely visible: difficulty in reaching
  spiritual enlightenment
- Clear lines that are as "fine as strands of silk": intelli-
  gence and good organizing skills
- Fuzzy deep lines: stupidity and poverty
- Reddish lines: generally favorable
- Pale yellowish lines: generally unfavorable

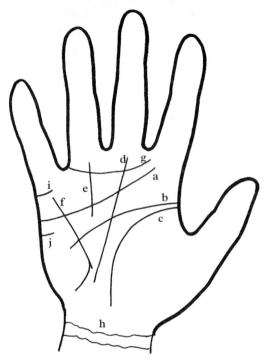

Figure 21.13: The Lines on the Hand

a-The Line of Heaven
b-The Line of Man (People Line)
c-The Line of Earth
d-The Column of Jade
e-The Line of Happiness
f-The Line of Greeting the Minister
g-The Line of Superior Help
h-The Jade Bracelet
i-Line of First and Second Wives
j-Line of a Single Species

- Very dark brown or black lines: sign of illness or approaching death

The Lines of the Hand

In traditional Chinese palmistry, there are three major lines and five minor ones. The major lines include the Heaven Line, The Line of Man (or "People Line"), and the Earth Line. Minor lines include the Jade Column, the Line of Happiness, the Greeting to the Minister line, the Line of Superior Help, and the Jade Bracelet. Two minor lines include the Line of First and Second Wives and the Line of a Single Species. These lines can be seen in Figure 21.13.

The Line of Heaven

For the ancient Chinese, the stars and all the heavens were believed to be a source of energy that gives life to both the human heart and spirit. The Line of Heaven, which corresponds to the heart line in Western palmistry (Figure 21.13a),

Figure 21.14: Short and straight Line of Heaven

reflects humanity's noble or vile tendencies.

Generally speaking, the longer and clearer the Line of Heaven, the more noble the person. A short line (for example, a line that reaches only as far as the middle finger) reveals a person who is basically selfish and dishonest.

Figure 21.15: Curved Line of Heaven

- Short, straight line ending under middle finger (Figure 21.14): difficulties early in life; no inheritance from ancestors; often rejected by others; jealous temperament

- Curved line ending at base of middle finger (Figure 21.15): famous father (such as well-known businessman, entertainer, or government official)

Figure 21.16: Line ending between index and middle fingers

- When line ends between index and middle fingers (Figure 21.16): difficulty maintaining primary relationship; difficulty holding onto money ("easy come, easy go")

- When line moves across the palm ending under the index finger (Figure 21.17): lucky in love, romantic, loyal

- When line moves completely across the palm and touches earth and people lines (Figure 21.18): high achiever in youth; troubles in relationships; difficult marriage

- Heaven line beginning low on the hand (Figure

Figure 21.17: Line of Heaven ending under index finger

Figure 21.18: Line touching earth and people lines

21.19): person tends to fall in love very easily; can be enthusiastic at first and then lose interest; success in business towards middle age; father will be generous

- A fretted Heaven line (Figure 21.20), known as the "Tails of the Phoenix": happiness and wealth, including inheritances from ancestors. However, if line is broken, this good fortune is negated
- Small vertical line from Heaven line to middle finger (Figure 21.21): money, knowledge, high intelligence
- Small vertical line from Heaven line to ring finger (Figure 21.22): artistic ability

The Line of Man (People Line)

The ideal man in early Chinese tradition symbolized the essence of intelligence. As opposed to a person ruled by the emotions, he was a personification of calm analysis and reason. This is why the Line of Man (Figure 21.13b), which corresponds to the head line of Western palmistry, reveals the ability to make decisions that are based on careful observation and rational thought.

As with other lines of the hand, the longer and clearer the Line of Man, the greater the intellectual abilities. A long line would bring wealth and good fortune to the owner, because it would reveal the ability to make correct decisions. A short, weak and/or broken head line was regarded

Figure 21.19: Heaven line
beginning low on the hand

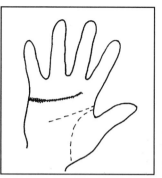

Figure 21.20: Fretted line of
Heaven

Figure 21.21: Vertical line to
middle finger

Figure 21.22: Vertical line to
ring finger

as a sign of poor intelligence and weak reasoning abilities; it could also mean that the person would be governed by the emotions, which could lead to making incorrect choices. A life of hardship and poverty would often result.

- A fretted or chained line (Figure 21.23): pessimistic nature, sly and crafty; propensity to illness
- Dots on the line (Figure 21.24): mental illness; suicidal tendencies; misfortune in business
- Long line curving downwards (Figure 21.25): the person tries his or her best in situations; tendency to be easily deceived by others

Figure 21.23: Fretted People line

Figure 21.24: Dots on People line

- Short and strong People line (Figure 21.26): honest, direct, faithful; individuals comfortable with what they have; liking for strong physical labor; sign of low economic status

- Line ending in a small branch (Figure 21.27): person take time to make decisions

Figure 21.25: Long People line curving downwards

Figure 21.26: Short, strong People line

Figure 21.27: Line ending in small branch

- Earth line and short, broad People line separated at commencement (Figure 21.28): person is willful and capricious; delinquency and criminality (depending on other signs on the hand)

- Earth line and People line separate at commencement with People line dropping towards Palace of Heaven (Figure 21.29): person will lose family inheritance; tendency to be unable to finish what one begins

- Earth line separate from People line, with people line

Figure 21.28: Separate Earth and People lines (I)

Figure 21.29: Separate Earth and People lines (II)

Figure 21.30: Separate Earth and People lines (III)

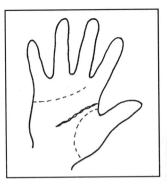

Figure 21.31: Chained People line

straight and long (Figure 21.30): self-made man or woman; capable and intelligent; possible strong temper

- Chained People line (Figure 21.31): low intelligence; poor memory; prone to headaches
- Islands on People line (Figure 21.32): pessimistic nature; instability in one's career and economic situation
- Small line parallel and above the end of People line (Figure 21.33): optimistic nature
- Break in People line with overlap (Figure 21.34): accident affecting the head

Figure 21.32: Islands on People line

Figure 21.33: Parallel lines above end of People line

Figure 21.34: Break in People line with overlap

Figure 21.35: Break in People line without overlap

- Break in People line without overlap (Figure 21.35): danger of death from disease or accident during "vulnerable" year in 12-year astrological cycle.

Note: Chinese astrologists believe that when people reach the year of their birth sign (Year of the Tiger, for instance, or Year of the Rat), every twelve years, they are especially vulnerable to death or disease. A break in the people line indicates that special efforts (such as praying, attending temple ceremonies, giving money to the poor, and doing other good deeds) should be undertaken to help prevent such events from taking place during that year.

The Cut

This rare line (Figure 21.36) corresponds to the Simian line in Western palmistry. The Chinese believe that this line is a sign of misfortune and hardship regarding the family. If found in the right hand, it indicates that one's mother will die early; if the Cut is on the left hand,

Figure 21.36: The Cut

the father will die early. When on both hands, this line reveals that one will not get along with siblings, resulting in separations and feuds.

The Line of the Earth

The Chinese have always viewed the earth as a source of fertility and vitality. The Earth line, which corresponds to what Westerners call the Life line, is related to birth, growth, and death (Figure 21.13c). It governs longevity, accidents, health, and disease. To the degree that the line is deep, long and clear, good health and long life are indicated. As with the Western interpretation of this line, a poorly formed, short, or broken line can indicate poor health, disease, and accident.

Peculiarities can have other meanings. For example, when the line does not begin at the thumb joint, it is considered a sure sign that the person is greedy and withholding.

- Broken line with overlap (Figure 21.37): recovery from disaster

- Broken line with two overlaps (Figure 21.38): always protected from major illness or financial reversal

- New jade line covering a break (Figure 21.39): help from others; whenever the person has a problem, he or she is rescued.

- Cross on the Earth line (Figure 21.40): prone to bad

Figure 21.37: Broken earth line with overlap

Figure 21.38: Broken earth line with two overlaps

Figure 21.39: New jade line covering a break

judgment; presence of this sign bodes poorly for doing business with relatives.

- Dot on Earth line (Figure 21.41): presence of illness that is not easily diagnosed; legal problems

- Small lines moving down from Earth line (Figure 21.42): in a

437

Figure 21.40: Cross on Earth line

Figure 21.41: Dot on Earth line

man's hand, abundance of physical strength and vitality; strong sex drive. In a woman's hand, poor health and low sex drive

- Line moving from Earth line to base of ring finger (Figure 21.43): person gets along well with others; attracts members of the opposite sex who provide help and support; good fortune in old age
- Line moving from Earth line to base of little finger (Figure 21.44): successful in business; intelligence and determination.

Figure 21.42: Small lines
moving down from Earth line

Figure 21.43: Line from Earth
line to base of ring finger

Figure 21.44: Line from Earth
line to base of little finger

The Column of Jade

The Column of Jade (also known as the Heavenly Column and Heavenly Happiness) is related to the Fate or Destiny line. In its perfect form, it moves upwards from the base of the hand near the wrist towards the middle finger (Figure 21.13d).

Like other lines in the hand, the Jade Column was

believed to be the result of our actions from previous lives, as well as from the actions of our ancestors. The presence of this line implies that our ancestors are protecting us, which would bring happiness, heavenly protection, and peace.

The Chinese believed that when this line moves in a straight path from the Palace of the Pit into the Palace of Separation, the owners will enjoy wealth, prestige, and overall happiness throughout their life. In addition, such a line indicates good health and longevity. In a sense, this long line is considered a sign of "communication with heaven," giving the individual a taste of what heaven has to offer.

If those possessing this line receive a good education in arts and letters, they are likely to achieve great fame. If uneducated and poor, they will become self-made men and women and be able to support a family.

To the degree that the line is weak, short, or broken, the person will encounter obstacles and misfortune. An absent Column of Jade is considered a certain sign of misfortune and a life of poverty.

- Line moving from Palace of the Pit to the base of the middle finger (Figure 21.45): in a man's hand, a sign of wealth and very long life. In a woman's hand, she will be a widow, although she will have many children and her husband will leave her money

- Line moving from Palace of the Pit to the middle of the Palace of Separation (Figure 21.46): a high eco-

Figure 21.45: Jade column
reaching base of middle finger

Figure 21.46: Jade column
reaching Palace of Separation

nomic and social position; happy marriage and good
relationship with one's children; long life

- Line moving from Palace of the Pit to the Heaven
  Line (Figure 21.47): if the person has a successful
  business, it will go bankrupt; if the person has a successful marriage, it will end; tendency to have problems getting along with parents

- Line moving from the Palace of the Pit to People
  line (Figure 21.48): talent, but thwarted by outer circumstances; difficulty with parents

- Line moving from the Palace of the Pit to the lower
  middle part of the palm (Figure 21.49): good health;

Figure 21.47: Jade column
reaching to line of Heaven

Figure 21.48: Jade column
reaching to People line

positive outcomes; easy to meet people who will provide assistance and support

- Wavy Column of Jade (Figure 21.50): business, friendships, and social position will experience many ups and
downs; improvement possible in middle age, but only
through hard work; person needs patience to overcome
adversity

- Overlapping break on line (Figure 21.51): failure in
friendships and business; vulnerable to illness and
danger

- Branch from line to base of index finger (Figure

Figure 21.49: Short jade column

Figure 21.50: Wavy jade column

Figure 21.51: Overlapping break on line

Figure 21.52: Branch to base of index finger

21.52): strong, combative personality; mark of a self-made man or woman

- Branch from line to joint between index and middle fingers (Figure 21.53): danger of losing one's economic and social position
- Line beginning in Palace of the Sky and moving to base of middle finger (Figure 21.54): strong personality with ability to attain high social and economic position; ability to attract support from others in high positions; support from previous three generations of ancestors
- Line beginning in Palace of the Sky and ending

Figure 21.53: Branch to joint between index and middle fingers

Figure 21.54: Line moving to base of middle finger

between lines of Heaven and People (Figure 21.55): success in life only through strenuous effort

- Line beginning in Palace of the Pit and ending at the base of the index finger (Figure 21.56): a difficult youth; stubborn and tenacious personality; can lose money easily

- Line beginning inside Earth line and moving to base of middle finger (Figure 21.57): help from one's mother; success in business

Line of Happiness

Closely associated with the Apollo line, this line begins

Figure 21.55: Line ending between lines of Heaven and People

Figure 21.56: Line ending at base of index finger

445

Figure 21.57: Line moving from Earth line to middle finger

Figure 21.58: Long and unbroken line of Happiness

in the center of the hand and moves towards the ring finger (Figure 21.13e). Considered a very good line to possess, the Line of Happiness reveals a pleasant life free of scandal or misfortune, as well as the probability of becoming prosperous and respected. It also is a sign that the individual is charitable in nature and generous to the poor.

- Long and unbroken line (Figure 21.58): intelligence; good friends; wealth

- Double Happiness line (Figure 21.59): strong and determined; attracts help from others; successful in business and marriage; good relations with one's children

Figure 21. 59: Double line of
Happiness

Figure 21.60: Weak, broken
line of Happiness

- Weak or broken line (Figure 21.60): many business
  and career reversals; tendency to misjudge situations
  and make mistakes

Line of Greeting the Minister

This line moves upwards from the Palace of Heaven towards
the Palace of Happiness (Figure 21.13f). It is related to the
line of intuition in Western palmistry, and, when long and
clear, is a sign of a highly evolved individual or a pure and
noble character. It also reflects powerful self-expression and
high moral ideals. However, when broken, this line may
reveal a promiscuous nature, with the potential of many

lovers.

Line of Superior Help

The line of Superior Help is known in Western palmistry as the Girdle of Venus. Whenever this line exists, Chinese palmists teach that it is a sign of virility. A clear and unbroken line (Figure 21.13g) can indicate an early marriage and success in relationships in general, while an indistinct, broken girdle reveals wealth early in life with bankruptcy towards middle age.

The Jade Bracelet

The Jade Bracelet is synonymous with the Rascettes of Venus, and indicates good health and good fortune (Figure 21.13h). Ideally, the bracelet should be formed by at least one clear and unbroken line, which indicates success in life. If the line is broken or fretted, the person may have difficulty achieving happiness and success in life. A series of three clearly marked bracelets was considered very auspicious among the early Chinese, indicating great good fortune and a long, healthy life.

Line of First and Second Wives

Presumably found in the hands of both men and women in ancient China, these lines correspond with the lines of union in Western palmistry. Found on the percussion of the hand under the little finger (Figure 21.13i), they indicate life partners and other major romantic relationships. As opposed to Western palmistry, which teaches that the earlier the relationship, the closer the line appears to the heart line, the Chinese believe that the first relationship is found closest to the little finger.

Like practitioners of Western palmistry, Chinese palmists believed that the longer and clearer the line, the deeper and longer the relationship. However, whenever a line moves across the Line of Heaven into the Palace of Happiness (Figure 21.61), early palmists taught that there would be secret relationships with one's servants in addition to one's marriage partner. Today, this interpretation would probably be amended to include all extra-marital relationships.

- Two parallel lines (Figure 21.62): two marriages
- Wavy lines (Figure 21.63): late marriage (in late 30's, at least); difficulty in relationships

Line of a Single Species

This line has no corresponding marking in Western palm-

Figure 21.61: Line moving into Palace of Happiness

Figure 21.62: Two parallel marriage lines

Figure 21.63: Wavy marriage line

istry. It consists of a single line along the percussion of the hand in the Palace of Happiness under the Heart line (Figure 21.64).

Its presence has several interpretations in Chinese palmistry. Some believe that it means that the individual will never marry, but focus the devotion and attention that would usually go to a

450

Figure 21.64: Line of a Single Species

wife or husband on friends, parents, siblings, and nephews and nieces. It is for this reason the line is sometimes said to indicate homosexuality. Two or more lines are said to indicate a strong love of children, though not necessarily in a sexual sense.

22

SIGNS AND SYMBOLS ON THE HAND AND FINGERS

The ancient Chinese believed that the union of several tiny lines formed different signs and symbols that could be found on the palm and fingers of the hand. They were thought to appear and disappear at different times during one's life, and could have different meanings depending on their location in the hand. Some signs appear as stars, triangles, and circles, while others have the appearance of early Chinese words, such as "woman" or "fire." (Many ancient pictographs have changed over the years, so they may have different meanings in China today.) Many have colorful names like "violet tortoise," "elephant's eye," and "jade stairway."

A Chinese palmist had to be highly skilled in locating and interpreting these signs, because some of them were regarded as extremely important: several could be a sure sign of approaching death. The form of the signs is rarely perfect, and they are not easy to identify. A few of them have been discussed in earlier chapters. However, on the following pages we'll examine some of the most common signs and symbols found in traditional Chinese palmistry and learn to appreciate their meanings.

The Animal (Figure 22.1)

This symbol corresponds to the ancient pictograph for "animal" in Chinese. It is a sign that the person will achieve a high position in life, especially in his or her career.

The Bracelets (Figure 22.2)

These are tiny, deep circles that leave an obvious impres-

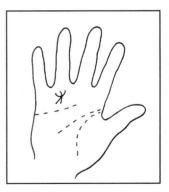

Figure 22.1: The Animal

sion in the skin. Wherever they are found, they signify good fortune. When reddish in color, they assure wealth.

Figure 22.2: The Bracelets

The Chess Board (Figure 22.2a)

The chess board is very similar to what Westerners call the grille. Yet contrary to the often negative meanings the grille has in Western palmistry, here it brings honors and wealth wherever it is found, with two exceptions: the Palace of the Mountain and the Palace of the Sky. When found in the former, the person will have constant frustration and sadness, unless already established in a stable profession. When found in the Palace of the Sky, the individual is overly-analytical and a con-

Figure 22.2a: The Chess Board

stant worrier. If other signs in the hand are unfavorable, the person may also be suicide-prone.

The Coffin (Figure 22.3)

When found in most parts of the hand, the coffin is a sign of a rather closed-minded person with a dour, boring personality. People with this sign have trouble achieving success in life due to limited perspectives.

Figure 22.3: The Coffin

However, when found in the Palace of the Mountain, in the lower part of the Venus mount, provided that it is completely formed and clearly visible, the coffin is a sign of approaching death. If the person's nails have turned black-ish as well, traditional Chinese doctors would say that he or she will be "sick in the morning, dead by the afternoon."

Confucius' Eye
(Figure 22.4)

Found on the thumb joint, it is a very clear oval. This is a sign that the person loves literature and the arts, and will likely attain a high degree of cultural sophistication.

The Crescent Moon (Figure 22.5)

The presence of this symbol in most places on the hand will bring the person good fortune and renown; however, when located on the lower two phalanges of the middle finger, it indicates death during a long journey.

Figure 22.4: Confucius' Eye

The Cross (Figure 22.6)

When the Cross is found on the Palace of the Winds, the person will not be close to his or her family. However, it also indicates that the individual will likely receive important help from a person of the opposite sex.

If located in the center of the hand, the cross suggests

Figure 22.5: The Crescent Moon

456

the danger of injury or death by stabbing. Believing that this sign appears as the result of bad deeds in a past life, Chinese palmists advise people to avoid conflicts and try to perform as many good deeds as possible to minimize the dangers that the sign implies.

Figure 22.6: The Cross

Death of Property (Figure 22.7)

Appearing like a sergeant's stripes, this sign foretells the loss of one's property and eventual bankruptcy.

The Demon (Figure 22.8)

True to its name, this symbol has a negative meaning wherever it is found. Believed to appear only on the hands of the vilest of people, it is a sign of a thief or assailant.

Figure 22.7: Death of Property

457

Figure 22.8: The Demon

Figure 22.9: The Dot

Figure 22.10: The Double Well

The Dot (Figure 22.9)

In Chinese palmistry, dots take the form of tiny holes in the skin and are considered quite favorable.

The Double Well (Figure 22.10)

This sign is described as "two wells crossed by a single bar," and is a sure

Figure 22.11: The Elephant's Eye

Figure 22.12: The Extension

indicator of wealth and the high regard of others.

The Elephant's Eye (Figure 22.11)

Made up of an angular line with a small hook at the bottom, this sign is found on the hands of people who are loyal and honest.

The Extension (Figure 22.12)

Formed by a rectangle and a cross, this is a sign of honors wherever it is found.

The Eye (Figure 22.13)

Appearing in the center of the Reception Hall, it is a sign of a mystically oriented person who possesses strong psychic ability.

The Field (Figure 22.14)

A positive sign, the field is composed of a cross within a square. It is a harbinger of wealth, depending on the Palace in which it appears.

The Flying Needles (Figure 22.15)

Composed of several fine, straight, parallel, upward-moving lines, this symbol can be found in any part of the

Figure 22.13: The Eye

Figure 22.14: The Field

palm. When it is reddish in color, it foretells success, especially if the skin of the palm is soft. However, if it is crossed by one other line, there is danger of death from decapitation. If found on any of the phalanges of the middle finger, the person is likely to die while on a long journey.

The Jade Stairway (Figure 22.16)

Not to be confused with the Double Well (page 458), this sign has special meaning when located in the Reception Hall, the quadrangle in the center of the palm. Whenever it appears there, it reveals strong intellectual abilities and the potential for great wisdom. If this sign is found on other parts of the hand, it brings happiness and good luck.

Figure 22.15: The Flying Needles

Figure 22.16: The Jade Stairway

461

The Jealous Wives (Figure 22.17)

An unfavorable sign. No matter where it appears, it indicates that the person will be the subject of envy and gossip.

Kittens of the Willow (Figure 22.18)

This unusual symbol is made up of superimposed small lines set at an angle to each other. This symbol may contain up to four angular lines.

When found in the Palace of the Pit, these lines reveal a life filled with honors, wealth, and high official positions.

Figure 22.17: The Jealous Wives

Figure 22.18: Kittens of the Willow

The Lid (Figure 22.19)

Like the square in Western palmistry, the presence of this sign (formed by two lines joined at an angle, giving the appearance of a roof or the lid of a pot) has the ability to mitigate the unfavorable indications of other lines or symbols.

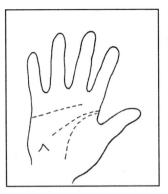

Figure 22.19: The Lid

Lines of Libertine Desires (Figure 22.20)

Not to be confused with the Flying Needles mentioned earlier, this symbol is formed by several squiggly lines found only on the Palace of Lightning or the Palace of the Mountain (the mount of Venus). People with these lines have very strong sexual and romantic desires throughout their life. One poet wrote that when these lines are present, "With the beginning of a new love, even a 90-year-old heart will be born anew."

The Lotus (Figure 22.21)

Formed by two separate lines, this symbol reveals strong religious tendencies, especially when found in the Reception Hall.

The Net (Figure 22.22)

Appearing like a Chinese fisherman's net of centuries past, this symbol is made up of a small circle with a sign of the moon located inside it. If found in the Palace of Separation, it indicates that the person will achieve a high position in government; if it appears in any of the other palaces, the person will achieve honor in the military.

Rat's Eyes (Figure 22.23)

Found in the Palace of the Pit, this sign portrays an individual who is greedy and covets things he or she may not even need. Often found on the hands of swindlers and thieves.

The Seal of the Golden Flower (Figure 22.24)

This positive symbol is essentially an eight-pointed star. It

Figure 22.20: Lines of Libertine Desires

Figure 22.21: The Lotus

Figure 22.22: The Net

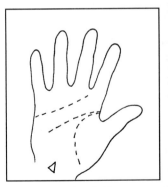

Figure 22.23: Rat's Eyes

brings strength and brilliance to those who have it on their hands. Its presence reveals a person with high aspirations, and assures wealth and happiness in life. People with this sign on their hands achieve high professional status that is the result of their own hard work and persistence.

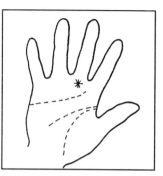

Figure 22.24: The Seal of the Golden Flower

The Seal of Gold
(See page 392.)

Known as the square in Western palmistry, this sign reveals honor and wealth wherever it is found.

- When located in the Reception Hall: good understanding and high scholarly achievement
- When found in the Palace of the Heavens: sign of a person of great wisdom

The Southern Star *(See page 399.)*

This unusual sign is formed by a group of five or more small holes arranged in a group.

- When found in the Reception Hall, the person will accumulate much property.
- When reddish in color (especially on a smooth palm), the person will become very wealthy.
- If found on the middle finger, it foretells death during a long journey.

The Suspicious Body
(Figure 22.25)

As you can imagine, this sign is a symbol of misfortune wherever it appears on the hand. It foretells suffering and ruin as the result of injustice.

The Triangle *(Figure 22.26)*

This sign is favorable everywhere except in the Palace of the Pit. When it appears

Figure 22.25: The Suspicious Body

Figure 22.26: The Triangle

in that Palace, it reveals a person who likes to steal and embezzle. When found elsewhere on the hand, it indicates that the person inspires confidence and can achieve influence in the community. As a result, he or she receives frequent promotions and becomes wealthy and powerful, often in middle age.

The Two Boats (Figure 22.27)

This unfortunate sign foretells disgrace and poverty no matter where on the hand it appears.

Union (Figure 22.28)

When situated beneath the index finger, this sign reveals that two families will live together in the same house. It also foretells that children born out of wedlock will bring prosperity to the home.

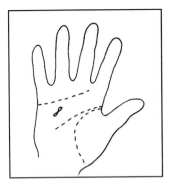

Figure 22.27: The Two Boats

Figure 22.28: Union

The Violet Tortoise (Figure 22.29)

Wherever found, it is a sign of success and renown.

The Well (Figure 22.29a)

When found in a male hand, this is a sign of a charismatic individual who will do very well in govern-

Figure 22.29: The Violet Tortoise

469

Figure 22.29a: The Well

Figure 22.30: The Wheel

ment service, politics, or business. If in a female hand, it indicates that she will marry into wealth.

The Wheel (Figure 22.30)

Appearing as a circle, this sign is considered favorable no matter where on the hand it is found. Generally speaking, it symbolizes the presence of an internal force that defends us from external dangers.

- If located on the thumb: intelligence
- If found in the Palace of the Earth: accomplishment through one's own efforts

- If seen in the Reception Chamber: mystical nature

The word "Earth" (Figure 22.31)

Chinese sages believed that people with this sign on their hands tend to be nosey, cruel, and tiresome to be with.

The word "Fire" (Figure 22.32)

This sign foretells fevers and seizures.

The word "Hands" (Figure 22.33)

It is a sign of a pure soul and loyal nature.

Figure 22.31: The word "Earth"

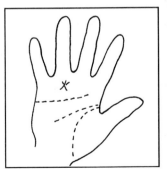

Figure 22.32: The word "Fire"

Figure 22.33: The word "Hands"

The word "Knife" (Figure 22.34)

This symbol foretells poverty and disgrace, no matter where it is found on the hand.

The word "Nail" (Figure 22.35)

This symbol indicates that we can never escape from difficulty or dangerous situations.

Figure 22.34: The word "Knife"

Figure 22.35: The word "Nail"

472

The word "Ten"
(See page 388.)

Not to be confused with the Cross, this favorable sign means success and good fortune wherever it appears, revealing that one's talents will lead to wealth and power. When found in the Reception Room, it implies having the protection of a powerful ally who will enable us to make lucrative deals and obtain wealth, even if our actions are questionable.

The word "Then"
(Figure 22.36)

No matter where on the hand this unfortunate symbol is found, it foretells that no matter how many things we try to accomplish in life, we always will fail.

The word "Woman"
(Figure 22.36a)

When found in a male hand, this symbol is a mark of sensuality.

Figure 22.36: The word "Then"

- When located in the Palace of the Earth:the person will have a human protector

- When found in the center of the palm: the person will establish a family

- When found on the index finger: a high position in life

Figure 22.36a: The word "Woman"

The word "Valley" (Figure 22.37)

A very favorable sign wherever it is found on the hand, the Valley signifies longevity. On the hands of men, it brings a rich and healthy old age. Among women, it foretells that they will receive great respect in their old age, "like a saint."

Figure 22.37: The word "Valley"

- If dark in color and found in the center of the palm: wealth
- Wherever it appears: many sex partners but few children

V

PRACTICAL
PALMISTRY

23

HOW TO READ HANDS

Hand Reading Technique

There is no single method or technique to reading a hand. I encourage readers to develop the method that works best for them, but the following general procedure may be helpful.

Preparation

- Before you are to read another's hand, try to become aware of both the privilege and the responsibility involved. Meditation and prayer are useful to help you become grounded in your "core" or higher self, and to come into closer contact with your intuition.

478

- Before you look at the person's hands, ask if he or she has ever had a reading before. Point out that the hands show tendencies and not always definite facts, and that the hands can change, even within a matter of weeks.

- Ask the person's age and find out if he or she is right- or left-handed. Explain that the passive hand is generally the storehouse of our potential, while the active hand more clearly expresses what we are doing with it.

Looking at the Hands

- Sitting directly across from the client, take both hands in yours and look at them. I close my eyes for a moment and say a silent prayer to help me focus and do my best. I ask simply, "Thy will be done," while a friend prefers, "I pray that all I may now tell him/her will be for his/her highest good and the highest good of all concerned." This momentary spiritual focusing need not be so obvious as to be noticed by the person who has come to you for a consultation, but can appear as though you are merely collecting your thoughts before proceeding with the reading.

- Look carefully at both hands. Take note of the size,

shape, skin texture, and flexibility. Note the positions and length of the fingers, taking into account the basic hand types. Don't be afraid to touch, bend, and squeeze the hands gently as you examine them.

- Observe the fingers carefully, taking special note of their size, flexibility, shape, and contour. Are any of the fingers bent? Which are prominent and which are weak? How are they "held" on the hand? In addition, take note of the skin ridge patterns on each of the fingertips. Use a magnifying glass if you need to.

- Turn the hands over and observe the nails, and ask the person to open the hands wide. Check out the knuckles as well as the relative position of the fingers to each other and to the hand as a whole.

- Turn the hand over again and examine the mounts. Run your finger over each mount and judge its relative strength. Note any markings on the mounts, such as squares, crosses, and grilles. Be aware of any specific skin ridge patterns between the fingers or on the mounts of Luna, Venus, or Mars.

- Look at the lines, taking careful note of their strength, clarity, and length. Where do they begin and where do they end? Are there breaks, dots, or islands on the lines? Are there branches or color changes? How do the lines differ on each hand?

After examining the hands for a few minutes, you will get a "feel" for them and a basic understanding of who the person is that you are reading.

- Take the active hand and begin reading, being ready to look at the passive hand for confirming or contrasting traits. Begin the reading at whatever point feels most appropriate. With some people, you may decide immediately to discuss health issues, while with others you might begin with some observations about character or career. You may also prefer to simply go over the hand features one by one. Use your judgment.

- Continue your reading, being sure to cover all areas of interest including health, life history, emotional characteristics, career, travel, relationships, and other aspects like creativity and spirituality. Proceed slowly, always being open to intuitive messages from your subconscious.

- Don't forget to make frequent eye contact with the person whose hands are being read.

- You may prefer to answer questions during the reading itself, or ask for questions when you are done.

Throughout the reading, try to keep the following issues in the back of your mind and ask yourself if you are dealing with them:

- What is the person really looking for?

- What is she/he ready to hear?

- Is what I am saying appropriate for this person at this time?

- What is the best approach to help this person develop his/her sense of initiative, responsibility, and participation in life?

- Does the reading touch on sensitive issues of my own that may affect the reading and my objectivity?

- Am I making myself clear and am I being understood?

At the conclusion of the reading, people often ask questions like "Will I get married (or divorced)?" "How many children will I have?" and the classic "When am I going to die?" Since the hands show probabilities and therefore can change, make it clear that any specific prediction is pure guesswork. As we mentioned earlier in the text, *never* predict the time of death, especially since you will probably be wrong anyway.

When practiced with care, sensitivity, and humility, hand analysis can be an endless source of adventure, learning, and inspiration. By helping others increase their self-knowledge, we invariably deepen our own. By helping others "remove the stones from the path," we open our own channel for compassion and service.

24

HOW TO TAKE HANDPRINTS

One of the best ways to deepen our understanding of the hand is to maintain a record of the hands we analyze. One way is to make plaster casts, but although they faithfully show hand shape and lines, they are complicated to make and extremely difficult to store. Photographs of the hands are simple to take and store, but often involve considerable expense. Photocopy machines and scanners often miss small lines and markings.

The easiest and cheapest method of recording hands is taking palm prints. Although the prints don't always reveal the exact hand shape, lines and skin ridge patterns can be faithfully reproduced, especially after some practice.

When used in conjunction with the Hand Analysis Test

Chart described later on, a collection of handprints can be very useful. In addition to providing a permanent record of the hand itself, subsequent follow-up prints can reveal changes in the hands over the years.

Materials

The materials needed for taking hand prints are both inexpensive and easy to obtain:

- A rubber roller approximately four inches (10 cm) wide
- A tube of black water-base block printing ink. In my opinion, the best ink available is manufactured by Daler-Rowney in England, although "Speedball" brand ink is suitable and may be more easily found in the USA and Canada
- Good quality art paper. You may prefer single sheets, or a spiral-bound art book for easier storage
- A thin pad of foam rubber or a tea towel to provide a suitable cushion for the paper
- A sheet of glass, linoleum, or newspaper for applying the ink. An old newspaper is most convenient, but the paper tends to absorb the ink

Procedure

- First, lay the paper over the foam rubber, which helps mold the paper so that it conforms to the contours of the hand. Roll out the ink on the glass, linoleum, or newspaper (Figure 24.1).

- Carefully ink the subject's hand, using just enough ink to lightly cover the entire palmar surface (Figure 24.2).

- Have the subject place his or her hand on the paper in a natural way, without intentionally opening or closing the fingers.

Figure 24.1: Rolling out the ink

Figure 24.2: Applying the ink to the palm

- Apply pressure to the entire hand (paying special attention to the center of the palm and the space between the finger mounts) in order to obtain a complete impression (Figure 24.3).

- You may also want to carefully outline the hand in pencil to record the approximate shape of the hand.

- Hold the paper to the table as the hand is slowly withdrawn. This will prevent the print from blurring. The finished print will be dry in several minutes (Figure 24.4).

Figure 24.3: Applying the hand to the paper

Figure 24.4: The finished print

In addition to the print itself, it's a good idea to include a record of the major features of the hand, such as the shape, dominant fingers, and mounts, as well as personal data concerning the individual whose print you are including in your collection. A suggested Hand Analysis Test Chart is included here for your convenience.

HAND ANALYSIS
TEST CHART

NAME: _____

DATE OF BIRTH: _____

TODAY'S DATE: _____

PREDOMINANT HAND TYPE: _____

STRONGEST MOUNTS _____

WEAKEST MOUNTS _____

TESTS:

SKIN TEXTURE _____

SKIN COLOR _____

FLEXIBILITY _____

CONSISTENCY _____

FINGERS (DESCRIBE):

JUPITER

SATURN

APOLLO

MERCURY

PREDOMINANT

LONGER OR SHORTER THAN PALM

STRAIGHT

BENT

THUMB:

SIZE

FLEXIBILITY

HOW SET (HIGH, MEDIUM, LOW)

WILL PHALANGE (DESCRIBE)

LOGIC PHALANGE (DESCRIBE)

SKIN RIDGE PATTERNS:

THUMB _____

JUPITER _____

SATURN _____

APOLLO _____

MERCURY _____

ON THE PALM ITSELF _____

NAILS:

SIZE _____

SHAPE _____

COLOR _____

UNUSUAL FEATURES _____

ADDITIONAL COMMENTS/ PERSONAL DATA:

_____

_____

AFTERWORD

Hand analysis provides a master key to help us achieve self-awareness and understand our place in the universe. It teaches that each individual temperament is a unique, equal, and valid reflection of spiritual reality, and shows how it can be expressed in a positive and dynamic way from the core of our being.

It can guide us towards becoming aware of our hidden talents and aspirations, and can help us bridge the gap between our inner desires and outer reality. By taking responsibility for our life path, we can come into contact with what we really want on a deep level. Above all, hand analysis can inspire us to expand our inner vision. To the degree that we are able to release these positive unconscious forces, we are able to help others come upon their innate wisdom, joy, and inner peace.

ABOUT THE AUTHOR

A 1971 graduate of the University of Wisconsin, Nathaniel Altman first became interested in palmistry while studying political science in Bogota, Colombia in 1968.

The author of twenty published books on health, relationship and nature, his palmistry titles include: *The Palmistry Workbook* (Aquarian/Sterling, 1984 with eight foreign language editions), *Sexual Palmistry* (Aquarian/Harper Collins, 1986 with six foreign language editions), *Your Career in Your Hands* [with Andrew Fitzherbert] (Aquarian, 1988), *Medical Palmistry* [with Eugene Scheimann, M.D.] (Aquarian, 1989) and *Discover Palmistry* (Aquarian/ Harper Collins, 1991).

He has also been a featured consultant in several other works, including *Visions and Prophesies* (Time Life Books, 1988), The *Psychic Sourcebook* by Fred Levine (Warner Books, 1985) and *Psychic New York* by Patricia Campbell (City Books 1996).

A resident of Brooklyn, New York, Nathaniel Altman has traveled and lectured extensively throughout North America, Europe, Latin America, India and Australia. Over the years, he has appeared on over two hundred radio and television programs in the United States, Canada, Australia and Great Britain. He speaks fluent Spanish, as well as French and Portuguese.

INDEX

If you liked this book, you'll love this series:

• Little Giant Book of Optical Illusions • Little Giant Book of "True" Ghost Stories • Little Giant Book of Whodunits • Little Giant Encyclopedia of Baseball Quizzes • Little Giant Encyclopedia of Card & Magic Tricks • Little Giant Encyclopedia of Card Games • Little Giant Encyclopedia of Card Games Gift Set • Little Giant Encyclopedia of Dream Symbols • Little Giant Encyclopedia of Fortune Telling • Little Giant Encyclopedia of Gambling Games • Little Giant Encyclopedia of Games for One or Two • Little Giant Encyclopedia of Magic • Little Giant Encyclopedia of Mazes • Little Giant Encyclopedia of Palmistry • Little Giant Encyclopedia of Puzzles • Little Giant Encyclopedia of Superstitions • Little Giant Encyclopedia of Toasts & Quotes • Little Giant Encyclopedia of Travel & Holiday Games • Little Giant Encyclopedia of Word Puzzles • Little Giant Encyclopedia of the Zodiac

Available at fine stores everywhere.